The American Tradition
in Foreign Policy

THE
AMERICAN
TRADITION
IN
FOREIGN
POLICY

by

FRANK TANNENBAUM

☆

UNIVERSITY OF OKLAHOMA PRESS

NORMAN

By FRANK TANNENBAUM

Labor Movement (New York, 1921)
Wall Shadows (New York, 1922)
Darker Phases of the South (New York, 1924)
Mexican Agrarian Revolution (New York, 1928)
Peace by Revolution (New York, 1933)
Osborne of Sing Sing (Chapel Hill, 1933)
Whither Latin America? (New York, 1934)
Crime and the Community (New York, 1938, 1953)
Slave and Citizen (New York, 1947)
The Struggle for Peace and Bread (New York, 1950)
A Philosophy of Labor (New York, 1951)
The American Tradition in Foreign Policy (Norman, 1955)

Library of Congress Catalog Card Number: 55–6364

Copyright 1955 by the University of Oklahoma Press
Publishing Division of the University
Composed and printed at Norman, Oklahoma, U.S.A.
by the University of Oklahoma Press
First edition, March, 1955
Second printing, September, 1956

To Carlton J. H. Hayes
as a token of
my regard and appreciation

Acknowledgments

This book owes much to Robert Livingston Schuyler, now Professor Emeritus of English Constitutional History at Columbia University. The many talks we had about the main theme the volume carries, his wisdom, his wide knowledge, and his comments on the manuscript in its earlier form were of great value to me.

I gratefully acknowledge a grant from the Rockefeller Foundation which facilitated the completion of this as well as my previous volume.

FRANK TANNENBAUM

Contents

Introduction

A great debate on the character and purpose of American foreign policy has been precipitated by those who would persuade our people to abandon their humanitarian and pacific traditions and frankly adopt the doctrine of power politics and of the balance of power as the basis of their foreign policy. This doctrine is confessedly, nay gleefully, amoral. It prides itself upon being realistic and takes Machiavelli as its great teacher. It is contemptuous of the simple beliefs of honest men, jeers at the sentimentalism of those who believe that men may strive for peace among nations, and looks upon democracy as a hindrance to skilled diplomacy. It looks with a certain derisive superiority upon the great leaders of this nation from Thomas Jefferson and John Quincy Adams to Woodrow Wilson and Franklin Delano Roosevelt, describes them as moralistic and sentimental, and suggests that our models ought to be Richelieu, Clemenceau, and Bismarck. Its adherents believe that international wars, instead of being made by men and supported by institutions humanly contrived, have their origin in the nature of man himself and are inevitable. The best they foresee is an armed balance of power—until the next war. And after that, more skilled diplomacy towards the achievement of the same inevitable end, a new balance of power ending in a new war. This dreadful doctrine has now won wide acceptance among teachers of international relations in many of our largest universities. It has become the *science* of international relations—and who would quarrel with science, especially when it comes packaged in good clear English and from high sources? But it is not science. It is make-believe. Its "scientific" basis is false and spurious. It is, in fact, only poor logic based upon deceptive promises, and its claim to be a science is just a bit of unholy conceit. For what we are dealing with is not a tentative hypothesis put forth by humble men as possible clues for other students to analyze, criticize, modify, and reject—or partially accept. No, we are offered a doctrine for national behavior which runs counter to the very essence of the American tradition and are told to accept it in the name of the national interest because their science has discovered what that interest is.

This debate is of greater import to the future of the United States than the old argument between the "interventionists" and the "isolationists." Both of them accepted the traditional American belief in international good will, in the doctrine of friendship among nations, in the right of the little nation to abide in security and without fear, in the hope of finding a way to peace among nations, in the sanctity of international treaties, in the belief in international law, and in the hope that the democratic way, by enhancing human dignity and widening human freedom, would ease the burden of conflict among men and nations. The "interventionists" and "isolationists" differed about how best to effectuate these ideas into formal policy, but they did not, with strikingly few exceptions, repudiate the doctrines that this nation has lived by from its very inception.

Now the advocates of *realpolitik* would sweep away all of our old beliefs as foolish, sentimental, and moralistic. They would have us build our future upon the concept of the balance of power in international relations, throw all morality and law out of the window as a nuisance and hindrance to skilled diplomacy, divide the world between Russia and ourselves, repudiating our past beliefs, as well as the promises, the obligations, and the treaties that bind us to our many allies, and girdle ourselves with a permanent and huge military establishment—for what?—to carry the happy game of skilled diplomacy from one war to the next. Most of this is explicitly stated in the argument. Some of it is implicit and constitutes a challenge to the democratic process itself. These doctrines, if adopted and implemented, would convert the United States into a centralized military empire and in due time would destroy the democratic institutions under which this government has lived and prospered these many years.

The debate is just beginning. A good deal more will be heard of it in the next few years. The American people cannot act upon this advice without ceasing to be either a Christian or a democratic people.

This essay is an attempt to state what has always been the American philosophy of international relations. It brings to the surface the beliefs and the ideals upon which this nation was built as a great federal system and shows how these same commitments have shaped our foreign policy from the beginning. The fact that so erudite a scholar as Professor Hans J. Morgenthau of the University of Chicago, and so subtle a mind as George F. Kennan are the chief proponents of the doctrine of *realpolitik* in the United States will add zest to the debate.

We must be clear what the debate is about. One side

believes that it is necessary, nay inevitable, that the relations between nations be built upon the principle of the balance of power. The other believes that it is possible and, if man wishes to save himself from destruction, desirable to organize international relations on the basis of the co-ordinate state. The first view derives its conclusions and its laws from the modern national-state system of Europe; the other from the experience of the federal system of the United States, from the development of the organization of American states, from the recent adoption of the principle of the co-ordinate state on which to frame the Commonwealth of Nations, and from the federal history of Switzerland. These two opposing conceptions of the basis of international organization carry with them underlying assumptions with respect to the nature of man and the possible role of human institutions, as well as implicit attitudes towards the democratic process.

Frank Tannenbaum

New York City
February 10, 1955

The American Tradition
in Foreign Policy

The American Commitment

IN a time of crisis such as the American people are now facing, it is necessary to re-examine the ground upon which our institutions are built, and look again at the faith with which they are imbued. These institutions, molded by time and experience, contain values that give meaning to the things we do. If we see the world differently from other peoples, it is because time, place, and fortune have wrought their own special imprint upon the American conscience, and endowed our folk with an ethical basis peculiarly their own. The indefinable something we call the American outlook adds up to a philosophy of life and a political morality. But Americans are inclined to take their ethical notions for granted and busy themselves with immediate issues. In the past, the people of the United States have not worried about their ideology and would not have recognized the meaning of the word if used to describe their beliefs. If, in the present crisis, Americans are troubled and confused by the contradictory policies urged upon them, it is because their counselors speak a language alien to the experience and indifferent to the inspiration of American polity. We have lost sight of the drift of our own history and of the sweep of its great energy.

This exuberant and restless power, so recognizably descriptive of the United States, has been disciplined by an equally strong moral bias which has not only contained it within bounds, but humanized it as well. How else explain that this crude and boundless might, which fought two great wars three and six thousand miles distant from its own shores, at the height of its military glory—with the enemy defeated and the world helpless to resist the strength of its armies—dismantled its gathered force and returned to the pursuit of peaceful ways, asking only that the other nations of the world do the same. It did this without making any demand for territory, for domain, or for special privileges. It placed no foreign people under duress, dictated no special government for other nations, and exacted neither homage nor obeisance from the weak, as well it might have done. More than that, it not only denied itself any compensation for the burden laid upon the American people by two wars, but at the end of the fighting, it offered its resources and skill to help bind the wounds and assuage the pain that the wars had inflicted upon other peoples, including the enemies it had helped to defeat.

The Hoover Commission in the First World War and the U.N.R.R.A. and Marshall Plan at the end of the Second World War are parts of the effort by the American people to make life livable again for those who suffered in these conflicts. Nor is this the end of the story. After the First World War, Wilson became the architect of a League of Nations that would protect the weak against the strong, and, during the Second World War, Roosevelt and Hull were the chief sponsors of the effort to repeat through the United Nations what Wilson had attempted after the First World War. To say that a people who on two such occasions behaved in this way has no philosophy of politics, no sense of direction, and no international policy is to speak the sheerest nonsense. What may be said is that it never elaborated its implicit values into a conscious doctrine. This, however, is an evidence of strength and vitality. A formal ideology is an unconscious apology, a claim for validity that needs to be defended. A vigorous, spontaneous life calls for no explanation and overflows any doctrine.

The drift of American policy, both internal and external, is clear enough if we will only look at it. If we have not looked at it in recent times, it is in part attributable to the distorted doctrines our generation and the one before it have been caught up in. Those doctrines are not descriptive of our behavior, and do not stem from American experience. We have—and our intellectuals and teachers are perhaps more guilty than others amongst us—permitted ourselves to be beguiled by ideas of economic determinism and power politics. We have attempted to explain American foreign policy on grounds in which we really do not believe because we do not act upon them. Our behavior is a standing contradiction of the theories we have been taught from books based upon the beliefs and practices of other peoples. And when, as has happened on occasion, our government, through the executive departments, has behaved as if the doctrines of power politics and economic determinism were true, the American people have repeatedly repudiated the policy, and forced a return to the traditional, though inadequately formulated, American belief that the little nations of the world have the same right to live their own lives as the powerful. In fact, our sympathy for the weak has always been greater than our admiration for the strong. The "big stick" formula of Theodore Roosevelt is an anomaly in our experience, was condemned by large numbers of Americans from the beginning, and was formally repudiated within a few years after his death. The Reuben Clark memorandum on the Monroe Doctrine, written inside the State Department in 1928, represents the official demise of the "big stick" theme in our foreign policy.

In short, the people of this country have always had a principle of foreign policy. The idea that has chiefly influenced American relations with other states came to the surface during the troubles that led up to the War of Independence, was the major cause of the Revolution itself, and, to use William H. Seward's phrase, ". . . is in reality the chief element of foreign intercourse in our history."

The controlling proposition in American foreign policy was clearly enunciated by James Madison in what he said some years after Independence about the relations between the American colonies and Great Britain before the Revolution:

"The fundamental principle of the Revolution was, that the colonies were co-ordinate members with each other and with Great Britain, of an empire united by a common executive sovereign, but not united by a common legislative sovereign. The legislative power was maintained to be as complete in each American Parliament, as in the British Parliament. And the royal prerogative was in force in each colony by the virtue of its acknowledging the King for its executive magistrate, as it was in Great Britain by virtue of a like acknowledgment there. A denial of these principles by Great Britain, and the assertion of them by America, produced the Revolution."[1]

Similar views were expressed by other leaders of the American Revolution. James Wilson had written in

[1] *The Writings of James Madison*, ed. by Gaillard Hunt (9 vols., New York, G. P. Putnam's Sons, 1900–10), VI, 373.

1774, "that all of the different members of the British Empire are distinct States, independent of each other, but connected together under the same sovereign in right of the same crown."[2]

Thomas Jefferson said in his autobiography, "I took the ground which, from the beginning, I had thought the only one tenable, which was that the relation between Great Britain and these colonies was exactly the same as that of England and Scotland after the ascension of James and until the union . . . having the same executive chief but no other necessary political connection."[3]

Benjamin Franklin had argued that "Supposing [that Parliament has] power to make no laws for us . . . the colonies would then be so many separate states, only subject to the same king, as England and Scotland were before the union."[4]

This idea was held to justify the claims for independence. And "the fundamental principle" as stated by Madison, ". . . that the colonies were co-ordinate members with each other and that . . . the legislative power was . . . as complete in each American Parliament, as in the British Parliament," has remained the unbroken popular theme in American foreign relations. It was this conception that ultimately made Rhode Island and Texas equal within our federal union.

The Pan-American system of co-ordinate states rests upon the same "fundamental principle," and to this idea we can ascribe the gradual evolution of the Monroe Doctrine from a unilateral to a multilateral policy. It ex-

[2] *Selected Political Essays of James Wilson*, ed. by Randolph G. Adams (New York, A. A. Knopf, 1930), 81, n. 44.

[3] *The Life and Selected Writings of Thomas Jefferson*, ed. by A. Koch and W. Peden (New York, The Modern Library, 1944), 10.

[4] Quoted in Herbert Agar, *The Price of Union* (Boston, Houghton Mifflin Co., 1950), 12.

7

plains the "hands off" injunction we imposed upon European powers in regard to the Western Hemisphere, and is the chief reason for the nonaggressive attitude in the Monroe Doctrine.

This "fundamental principle" was the keystone for our advocacy of the "open door" in China, as it was the justification for a continuing opposition to Japan. We accepted the challenge of a war in the Far East rather than yield the governing principle in our foreign policy. The American belief in the political equality and moral integrity of the state, or to repeat Madison's phrase, "co-ordinate members," and "complete . . . legislative power," sanctioned our participation in two world wars, as well as our effort to develop a League of Nations to expand ". . . the doctrine of President Monroe to the doctrine of the world . . . that every people should be left free to determine its own polity, its own way of development, unhindered, unthreatened, unafraid, the little along with the great and the powerful. . . ."[5]

This is President Wilson's version of the "fundamental principle" which Madison described as the chief cause of the War of Independence. But the same conception was also one of the important reasons for the rejection of the League of Nations. One need but turn back to the debate in the Senate to recognize that what defeated the League of Nations was, in no small degree, the conviction that America's belief in the co-ordinate membership of all states had been betrayed. It was this same ideal that took us into the Second World War, and inspired the attempt to salvage, through the United Nations, the old dream that had failed in the League. There is peculiar consistency in this notion of ours that the little nation has the same rights as the big one. Our quarrel

[5] *Congressional Record*, 64 Cong., 1 sess., 1743.

with Russia is founded on it. The Truman Doctrine is a modern version of the basic propositions of President Monroe; and our defense of Korea is explainable on the conviction that the only kind of world the American people can comfortably live in is one in which Korea has no more right to attack and dismember Russia than Russia has to attack and dismember Korea or Finland. We really believe that Ecuador and Haiti are "co-ordinate" with the United States, just as we believe that Poland and Bulgaria are "co-ordinate" with Russia. And it is this conviction that underlies President Eisenhower's statement that "We will never acquiesce in the enslavement of any people in order to purchase fancied gains for ourselves."[6]

To some, these American notions seem impractical and foolish. Influential scholars and counselors would have us abandon them. They suggest that we cease being childish and idealistic and recognize that the "national interest" and "national security" require us to become disciples of Machiavelli, take our lessons from Richelieu, Bismarck, or Clemenceau. The fact that Germany and Japan have committed national suicide by consistent adherence to these doctrines, and that other nations, who in their own way followed the same teachings, have been greatly weakened, seems not to dampen the eloquence of those who would persuade us to surrender the beliefs and practices by which we have lived and prospered from the beginning.

But the American people cannot accept this counsel. It runs against the grain of their experience. Our history is so unlike that of most of the other nations of the earth that we see things in a special light. In ways not readily describable, our conception of the relations between states is different from that which has governed the interna-

[6] *New York Times*, February 3, 1953.

9

tional behavior of most other great powers. American attitudes towards foreign policy derive from a unique historical experience. While the United States is culturally a child of Western Europe, and its religious and political ideas stem from the Hebraic-Christian and Greco-Roman tradition, it has been deeply influenced by the pervasive impact of the New World. The discovery, conquest, and gradual occupation of the American continent have shaped the European heritage into something markedly unlike its original form. Our view of the world is not European, and the difference explains the grounds upon which we would build our relations with the rest of the world.

American history begins as an act of repudiation and high adventure. At the outset, it involved the abandonment of Europe, the crossing of an unknown ocean, and the building of a new life upon an unexplored continent. Americans are deeply conscious of having been the architects of their own destiny, of having organized their own society, and of having established their own government on a new basis. James Monroe expressed this idea by saying, "The revolution . . . has put the entire government in the hands of one order of people only—freemen; not of noble and freemen. This is the peculiar trait in the character of this revolution."[7]

It is true, of course, that much in American political thinking can be traced to English experience, particularly to the Puritan Revolution and to the ideas of John Locke. But separation from Europe by the Atlantic Ocean and the impact of the New World influenced the growth of institutions and attitudes that were essentially non-European in character.

[7] Jonathan Elliot, *Debates on the Adoption of the Federal Constitution* (4 vols., Washington, published under the sanction of Congress, n.d.), III, 208–209.

The most obvious distinction between America and Europe lies in the presence of a feudal tradition in the second, and its nonexistence in the first. The failure of the feudal tradition to establish itself on this side of the ocean has meant that the American people were freed from what has remained the most pervasive feature of the European ethos in modern times. We can see this by noting some of the obvious aspects of the feudal design.

The feudal tradition is authoritarian. Feudalism glorified the knight in armor and cast a halo about the ideal of personal combat. It idealized personal fealty and expected the good knight to lay down his life for his immediate overlord. It assumed a world divided into fixed orders and defined the rank of each individual by his birth. The lord owned the domain and ruled it as his, and the right to transfer the territory, with its people, to others as a result of war, marriage, or treaty, remained unquestioned through hundreds of years. Alliances and counteralliances between kings, lords, and nobles were accepted ways in the relations among the ruling hierarchy. The memory and feeling of a formalized and traditionally structured society lies in the background of modern Europe and of much of the rest of the world, even if the specific content of the feudal institutions varied greatly from one area to another. For centuries, European society was confined within the limits of caste and status.

In international relations, security required martial strength, alliances with neighboring princes, advantageous marriages, and the contriving of balances of power to stabilize an essentially unstable political order. The growth of European monarchies was largely an expansion of this political design upon a broader scale. The subordination of the nobility to the king increased the military might of a given dynasty without changing the superior-inferior relationship between the ruler and the ruled, which was little affected by growth of large states. The large states, built by conquest and marriage, continued to abide in a world of personal and family alliances, armed and balanced against each other, seeking to enhance the prestige and increase the power of the governing royal family.

Many revolutions have passed over Europe and the rest of the world in the last few centuries, and the face of society has been greatly altered. But the implicit attitudes between man and man, the notion of class, the idea of being born to rule, the belief in alliances, the exaltation of military virtues, the right to dispose of the domain and the people, the belief in the notion of a balance of power between different states, the acceptance of war as a matter of course in the effort to keep the balance or enhance the power of the king—now become the state—survived. The ideas of the Hohenzollerns, of the Czars, of the Hapsburgs in 1914 were not so different from what they had been in 1814 or 1714. Even in France and in England, the rights of the states as imperial and colonizing powers were not entirely indifferent to the older tradition of being born to rule.

The many European revolutions have more notably changed the form of the society than they have modified its content. The traditional feelings, beliefs, attitudes, postulates, and ideals survived beneath the surface, and new laws were written on the implicitly given assumptions. The French destroyed the centralized monarchy of Louis XIV only to create the more centralized state of Napoleon and the French Republic. The Communists shattered the police state of Nicholas II only to establish the greater police state of Stalinist Russia. They could probably not do otherwise. That was the only way they knew. Their world was fixed for them by centuries of habituation that defined the spirit and substance of government, and described accepted ideas of the relations between nations.

The United States stands outside this tradition and does not understand it. More than that, the American people cannot even sense the inner compulsions that made it possible. We have never known a society where the ruling nobility were divinely ordained to govern. We have, except in a limited way in the South, not even known the meaning of class persistent through time. We have known little of personal political fealty, and when we did, it was to the temporary and not necessarily noble political boss. Our commitments have been of a different order. And if our society has greatly changed, its underlying attitudes and beliefs have persisted. The way of life and sense of relationship between man and man has been shaped by the adventure of settling a continent, and in turn shaped a rule of government among men who were equal among themselves. In our world, effective social stratification was never possible for long—not even for one full generation. This has, in turn, carried over into our conception of the government. The government belongs to us. We do not belong to it. We made the government; it is ours. It does not belong to the king because there is no king. It does not belong to the governor or to the president because he is our own creation.

Charles Pinckney of South Carolina expressed it in the following words: "We have been taught here to believe that all power of right belongs to the people . . . that our rulers are the servants of the people, amenable to their will, and created for their use. How different are the governments of Europe!"[8]

Iredell of North Carolina makes the government the deliberate creation of the people and subject to modification at their will. "The people are known with certainty to have originated it [the government] themselves. Those in power are their servants and agents; and the people, without their consent, may new-model their government whenever they think proper, not merely because it is oppressively exercised, but because they think another form will be more conducive to their welfare."[9]

Many unexpected things have happened to our society in the last hundred and fifty years, but the ingrained sense of values derived from the subjugation of a vast and almost empty continent has persisted. The adventure that began with abandoning a European home continued through three centuries of pushing back the wilderness, and has left its imprint upon the American ethos. In lieu of the persistent values that flow from the feudal tradition, we have the feelings and beliefs that stem from subduing and peopling a new land. The endless migrants who shed their prejudices and older habits in conquering vast plains and boundless forests, which would yield only to the stubborn and the hardy, and knew nothing of lords and ladies, forged a new and different set of values.

Walt Whitman has given inimitable expression to this American feeling:

> *I am of old and young, of the foolish as much as the wise;*

[8] Elliot, *Debates on the Federal Constitution* (4 vols., Philadelphia, J. B. Lippincott and Co., 1861), IV, 319.
[9] *Ibid.*, 9.

Regardless of others, ever regardful of others,
Maternal as well as paternal, a child as well as a man,
Stuff'd with the stuff that is coarse, and stuff'd with the
stuff that is fine;
One of the Great Nation, the nation of many nations,
the smallest the same, and the largest the same;
A southerner soon as a northerner—a planter nonchalant
and hospitable, down by the Oconee I live;
A Yankee, bound by my own way, ready for trade, my
joints the limberest joints on earth, and the sternest
joints on earth;
A Kentuckian, walking the vale of the Elkhorn, in my
deer-skin leggings—a Louisianian or Georgian;
A boatman over lakes or bays, or along coasts— a
Hoosier, Badger, Buckeye;
At home on Kanadian snow-shoes, or up in the bush, or
with fishermen off Newfoundland;
At home in the fleet of ice-boats, sailing with the rest and
tacking;
At home on the hills of Vermont, or in the woods of
Maine, or the Texan ranch;
Comrade of Californians—comrade of free northwest-
erners, (loving their big proportions;)
Comrade of raftsmen and coalmen—comrade of all who
shake hands and welcome to drink and meat;
A learner with the simplest, a teacher of the thought-
fullest;
A novice beginning, yet experient of myriads of seasons;
Of every hue and caste am I, of every rank and religion;
A farmer, mechanic, artist, gentleman, sailor, quaker;
A prisoner, fancy-man, rowdy, lawyer, physician, priest.
I resist anything better than my own diversity;
I breathe the air, but leave plenty after me,
And am not stuck up, and am in my place.

The American ethical concept is, therefore, the sum
of a European heritage, molded by the successes, failures,

beliefs, and aspirations that have come of centuries of pioneering in a new world. Everything that has happened to the American people, in all of its diversity, and through many generations, has gone into shaping the American attitude towards life at home and abroad. Fundamentally, it is a way of being rather than a doctrine and is difficult to classify or catalogue.

The best that we can do is to cull a recognizable body of commitments, mainly unconscious, which have characterized the American people's attitudes towards life. A commitment is a kind of inner compulsion. It is not a practice, nor even a policy. It is compelling without being a point of reference to a value system classified as doctrine. The American commitments may, at some hazard, be partially described as follows:

(1) *We are committed to the ordinary folk.*

Our folk hero is neither king nor prince, neither lord nor noble. He is not a man of great wealth, like Croesus, nor a great military leader like Napoleon. He is neither a philosopher like Confucius, nor a religious teacher like Buddha. He is the pioneer, or even more specifically, the cowboy. He is independent, free, resourceful, and bound to no man. He lives a life of adventure. He rides a horse, and is quick on the draw. He needs few worldly goods, knows no malice, is any man's equal, and is always ready to maintain the law and defend the weak, even at the cost of his own life.

(2) *We are committed to the idea that all men are equal.*

In our culture, all men are spiritually equal. Their personality may not be intruded upon or denied. Every man must be allowed to grow to his own full stature. No one must be denied access to the opportunities available in our world. We will endow no man with special privileges, and sanction no power to override the moral dignity of any man. When in practice we fall short of our ideals, as we often do, we testify to our sins by a bad conscience, and by the public avowal that we meant no evil.

(3) *We are committed to individualism.*

We believe that there is no substitute for the private experience of the individual. In our culture, insight, ingenuity, and the initiative which flows from it must come from what each man garners and makes meaningful out of his own efforts. We recognize that each man combines the varied strands in our culture so as to give him a peculiarly personal body of knowledge and a private wisdom that makes of every man a uniquely endowed being who may not be equated with any other, and must not be denied.

(4) *We are committed to a world of co-operative action.*

If private wisdom and insight is allowed to each individual, public policy must be shaped by open discussion and by compromise. We square our individualism with the common good by calling upon each person to contribute his special knowledge towards an acceptable decision. Just because we believe that the experience of the many is essential to an adequate understanding of any public difficulty, we call upon each to make his private experience available for the good of all. And we do this upon all questions. Few, if any, other societies in the world call so often upon each individual to give public utterance to the truth that is in him. Issues of public policy, no matter how trivial, are usually dealt with through semi-formal group discussion and decision. Americans are organized to do just this in tens of thousands of associations, clubs, trade unions, chambers of commerce, Red

Cross chapters, and societies for the prevention of cruelty to animals. We discuss every subject, vote upon every dispute.

(5) *We are committed to racial tolerance.*

In the last one hundred and thirty years, we have absorbed some forty million foreigners, who came from all parts of the world. Literally every people in the world has contributed to the growth of the American community. Into the make-up of the American population have gone many thousands of English, Irish, Scotch, Italians, Poles, Russians, Danes, Swedes, Finns, Bulgarians, Turks, Armenians, Spaniards, Jews, Greeks, Germans, Chinese, Negroes, Mexicans, and representatives of every other racial and linguistic group in the world. In the same community, often in the same industrial establishment, there have been, and there are, twenty different racial elements. After the first generation they are all Americans. A curious kind of cultural assimilation has pervaded our society and has bred a new race out of the diverse elements of the world.

While it is true that some people have been more resistant to absorption than others, it is also true that all elements have been proud of becoming Americans and almost pathetically insistent on shedding the evidence of their origin. Intermarriage and a common public school system have done their work so well that in the United States, for more than fifty years, the source of origin has almost completely evaporated as a cause of separateness. If special elements can be pointed to as a contradiction of what has been said, it is still true, however, that the process of absorption has been more rapid than the process of stratification. At the present rate of integration, an American, in the near future, will have so many diverse racial strands that separate identification will become meaningless. The Negroes have, for obvious reasons, been less readily subject to this process of physical incorporation, but anyone who would deny that it goes on, and at an increasing rate, is not really aware of the social forces in American life.

No significant group wants to remain outside the common fold. Everyone wishes to be a part of the whole. Our failure to complete the process of integration is caused by the shortness of time rather than by an absolute denial of a common identity. Our unity stems from our diversity.

(6) *We are committed to democracy as a way rather than a theory of government.*

American democracy is not commensurable with other democracies, and it is largely immune to exterior currents of thought and action. American democracy is a habit, a way of life, a process of social relationship. It is not fundamentally a theory of government; it is a method of government that derives its consent from each person governed—even from those who oppose the specific things that the government may do. One may, in our society, oppose all of the policies of the administration and yet believe in democracy, because the methods of achieving the defeat of the existing administration are also democratic. In a democracy, he who has a concern has a voice, and the voice of each counts for one—and only for one. The rest is a matter of counting. The right to a voice, the personal conscience in expressing it, the freedom to utter an opinion, even an unpopular one, and the honesty of the count are all essential elements of any democratic society. Underlying it is the belief that the experience of the many is more inclusive than the experience of the few, that the voice of the people is the voice of God, that what the people want is what they need.

There is the further belief that no one knows better than the people themselves what they need at the moment. In a democratic society it is just as important to possess the right to be wrong as the right to be right, for in any society where a wrong opinion cannot be uttered it is not possible for long to utter a right opinion. All of these elements exist wherever democracy is a habit, but American society contains elements that give the above special relevance.

(7) *We are committed to local self-government.*

Ours is not only a commitment to self-government, but to local government. The federal government rests upon forty-eight states, and each state rests upon many counties. Each county, in turn, is made up of a number of townships. Governmental authority runs from the smaller to the larger unit. The county is governed by the township, the state by the county, and the federal government from the states. This is true in spite of the recent growth of federal power. The county government must secure the consent of the township, and the state must secure the consent of the majority of the counties, and the federal government is in the hands of a Congress that is responsive to the claims of the representatives of Congressional districts that are located within the states, and to senators elected by the states. The most significant thing in American politics is not the powers of the presidency, but the powers of the local political machine. The Westchester County Republican administration can outlive repeated Democratic state governors, and the Democratic machine in Jersey City outlasts any number of unfriendly governments in Washington. The presidency rests upon the support of the local political organization. The presidential election and the president's control of Congress depend upon the loyalty of the local political machines. That is why the president has never secured full control over Congress—not even in an emergency. That is why there are always enough Democrats to help the Republicans to defeat a Democratic president, and vice versa.

That is also why the national parties are loose federations of local party chieftains. Our government has been stable just because the national political parties have been weak, and national parties have been weak in proportion to the strength of local political machines. Foreign observers are often misled when they note the preponderance of two political parties. They should note that in both the Democratic and the Republican parties there are elements so diverse that under different conditions a great variety of parties could be constructed out of them. That they have not been is due to two very distinctive elements in American life. The first is the fact that local issues can be fought out locally, the party label being significant only in its national aspects. A conservative Democrat from Mississippi and a radical Democrat from New York meet only on the national issues. The second is that third parties in the United States have been fluid and temporary. They have lasted long enough to demonstrate that they really represent a considerable element in the voting population, but as soon as that has become evident, the larger and older parties have tended to absorb them by taking over their programs. That happened with the Granger movement, with the prohibition movement, with the movement for old-age pensions, to mention but a few. The large parties, in spite of their seeming narrowness and definiteness, have survived only because, in the long run, they have been open to new groups of sufficient importance to become a factor in winning an election.

Part of this process is a kind of fluid economic democracy which has long pervaded American life. There is no economic interest that is not organized. There are large and frequently conflicting organizations of labor and innumerable organizations of capital, each seeking, and at times successfully, to influence public opinion in its favor. There are groups in favor of the tariff and groups opposed to it; importers oppose the manufacturers; water transportation interests are in conflict with the railways; the railways oppose road transportation; and all of these may object to air transport subsidies. Agricultural interests frequently clash with manufacturing interests and may even be sharply divided among themselves. The cane-sugar growers are in conflict with the beet-sugar growers, and both of these differ with the sugar importers. The fact is that there is a kind of divergence of interest in American life that is all pervasive. Each of these interests has its own organization; each in its turn influences and on occasion secures public favor and governmental aid; and each in turn affects the distribution of income of the American people. No one person, no one group, completely dominates the scene, and each group must be constantly on the watch to maintain its position. The effect of this upon the making of American democracy, a sensitive and responsive instrument of public policy, is great indeed. It makes for lack of consistency in politics, but it also makes for freedom and for a shift of power as immediate needs and pressures seem to require.

These contradictory forces demand equality before the law and a weighing of public as against private interest that gives the American judicial system, and the Supreme Court in particular, a place in our scheme of things that is difficult for strangers to understand. It also calls for a complete freedom of the expression of opinion.

No such complex economic and social structure could survive unless each interest could make itself heard, unless each grievance found a voice, unless each group could influence public opinion. Without freedom of speech, press, assembly, and organization, American democracy could not function. It may be said that freedom in that sense is as available in the United States as can be expected in a social structure as large, varied, and sectional as ours is. Occasionally and locally, an attempted constriction of public utterance takes place, but it has always been temporary. Freedom is essential to American economic and public life, and both the conservatives and radicals believe in it for themselves and, therefore, for others. But such great divergence can survive only upon the assumption that the end in government is not victory but compromise. That explains the good fellowship that follows a heated campaign for office; that is why no one assumes that defeat in a political campaign is the end of his program; that is why, the day after election, the preparation for the next election may be said to begin. With us democracy is a method. The American way is by compromise in little bits, by persuasion, by much talk and little bitterness; and if the next fellow is wrong today, we were wrong yesterday, though it is hard to admit. With us all political bargains are temporary, and all programs are for the day. No great battle is ever lost, and no great victory is ever won. When the day is over, and the new party comes to office, it continues the program that it denounced yesterday, largely because it would lose its adherents if it changed it.

(8) *We are committed to a nonhierarchical society.*

Neither class nor caste, nor special families dominate American life. We have no aristocracy. Those of our families who would draw an aristocratic mantle over themselves were born yesterday, and will have disappeared tomorrow. A list of the prominent leaders in American life would reveal that their fathers or grandfathers were farmers, peddlers, laborers, skilled mechanics, or lawyers' clerks who starved in boyhood and achieved standing by the grace of good fortune, personal ability, and the wealth of a growing industrial society. The record will also show that many of the aristocrats of yesterday have today shrunk back into the mass and are indistinguishable from them; for in American social life, the test of status is a test of immediate achievement. He who survives must do so by his own works. No one in America can long live on his past or on the past of his fathers. What you do—that is the touchstone of American life. There is a vertical flow in the United States that works both ways, and the movement upward of new elements is compensated for by a movement downward. While wealth may be important, it, too, is temporary. Many a wealthy family of yesterday is in poverty today, and the papers record, almost daily, the death in poverty of the scion of a wealthy family of a generation or two ago.

Each generation must justify the honor, confidence, and power it claims for itself. Our law will tolerate no exclusive privileged class, and our social milieu will only allow for distinctions that are open to the competent and deserving from all the strata in American life. Amongst us the immigrant child may become a mayor of a large city, a governor of a state, a member of the Senate, or of the Cabinet, a great industrialist, or a powerful labor leader. But his children must reveal the same gifts of character and genius if they are to retain honors and privileges their father had earned.

(9) *We are committed to the ideal of human well-being.*

We will speed a plane across the continent to save the life of a single child, raise large sums by private and public subscription to relieve the victims of an earthquake in Japan, of a flood in China, of yellow fever in Brazil. The work of the Rockefeller Foundation is but the most conspicuous of the many undertakings by Americans to save human life and ease human suffering. The large sums spent under the E.C.A., the promise implicit in Point Four are natural to our feeling of responsibility to the less favored. To share our worldly goods with those who need them, to give time and energy to relieve pain among the suffering, and to teach the illiterate is so much a part of ourselves as to be taken for granted. The Ford Foundation is but the most recent evidence of the commitment. But more typical are the unassuming efforts of thousands of small and large groups who have labored in these fields over many generations. The desire to better human life is, with us, a continuing moral and religious impulse.

(10) *We are committed to religious tolerance.*

There is more than religious freedom in the United States. There is almost a kind of religious inventiveness in the American community. Not only have the religious beliefs brought from the Old World been free to develop as they could, but a surprising number of American-born credos have risen and flourished. American ground seems to favor new forms of faith, and some of these have grown into large and influential religious societies. The Mormon and Christian Science churches are good examples of American religious inventiveness. There are, however, numerous small sects. The city of Los Angeles is famous for the variety and the number of religious faiths that are to be found there. Not only has every religion been free to flourish and grow, but every new religious form has found fertile ground. The conflict between the churches has taken the form of a competition for adherents. The denial of freedom of worship is practically nonexistent, and the few voices of opposition have been lost in the general indifference to the issue raised. In the United States the worship of God is so varied that men profess their faith in every kind of temple, in every tongue, and in almost every form. The semihysterical public baptisms among Southern Negroes, on one hand, and the stately formal ritualism of the Greek church, on the other, are but bare elements of a scale that runs as wide as the human imagination.

(11) *We are committed to dealing with issues as they arise.*

More important, perhaps, than any of the things said so far is the American commitment to "cross the bridge when we get to it." Our whole view of life is contained in the belief that "sufficient unto the day is the evil thereof." We can make no large plans for the indefinite future because we know intuitively that we can only work in the present. We know that our next step can only be taken from our present position, and that what we will be able to do tomorrow will be shaped by what we do today. To us, the means determine the ends. We design to do the things we can do, and these are shaped by the things we have already done. If we would estimate where we are heading, if we would get our sense of direction, we look backward and see where we came from. With us, the immediate is the ever present. With us, the future lies in what we can do now. Our competence, our power, and our values stem from past achievements rather than from promises of a future over which we know we have no control and could not harness even if we tried.

(12) *We are committed to the belief that evil is remediable.*

26

Our whole life is an effort to make things better, easier, more manageable. The concept of stagnation is abhorrent to our way of thinking. Change we take as given. Our sense of social, political, and industrial life is one of movement. Every agreement, every judicial decision, every law, every invention is recognized as a temporary point on a moving line. We stand between stagnation and cataclysm because the first is a denial of the living process, and the second is a destruction of it. The continuing effort to remedy the specific evil has made ours a dynamic culture. We take nothing for granted, we accept nothing as perfect, we define nothing as the final end. The automobile, the atomic bomb, the increase in the span of life, the vast growth in productivity, the keeping of millions of young folk in schools and colleges are all by-products of a devotion to doing the things that can be done.

(13) *We are committed against utopianism, dogmatism, formalism, and fanaticism.*

To us, a Utopia is a dream rather than a reality. Dogmatism is a denial of the living and infinitely variable social process. Formalism is an impediment to experimentation, and fanaticism a moral perversion. The "I am from Missouri" is descriptive of most Americans. The Utopian promise sounds like a "tall story." The dogmatic assertion is countered with the skeptical, "Is that so?" and fanaticism with the comment that all men may worship God in their own way, with the conviction that no man is always right, with the assertion that freedom and truth cannot be had where men are not permitted to be wrong in their effort to be right. We find unacceptable the doctrine that a belief in a future Utopia justifies the doing of present evil. To us, he who does evil in the name of some future good is possessed of evil.

To us, all formal doctrine for the shaping of human destiny in this world is contrary to experience because we know that the good life can only be had by doing the beneficent things that are within our immediate reach.

(14) *We are committed to the juridical and political equality of states.*

The implicit American foreign policy is the child of the fact that, in the United States, Rhode Island and Texas are equal. It is the child of that most remarkable political decision which induced the founders of our Republic to give the small and the large states an equal vote in the Senate, to divide the vast and unpopulated territories of the Northwest into states, and to admit them on an equal footing when they had satisfied certain minimum conditions of population and constitutional conformity. That was perhaps the most important single political decision in our history. It has made possible the organization of a vast continent under a single federal government. It has eliminated invidious distinctions between the states, and has made juridical and political equals of small and large political units.

These commitments—and they are an incomplete listing—are inherent in our way of being. In their sum they characterize American life and describe what might, by stretching a term, be called an American philosophy. They do not detail a policy or describe a practice. They are, somehow, in the background of any practice or policy. They are the elements of the American as contrasted with the remnants of the feudal tradition which is ingrained in European attitudes towards national and international life.

These idealized beliefs have not prevented us from all too often violating them. We have many times infringed upon our commitment to racial tolerance, denied the Negro equality before the law, scorned different religious practices, corrupted the popular suffrage, given special privileges to the wealthy, perverted the doctrine of equal opportunity, and bullied the weaker nation. We have been guilty of acts of commission, and more often, of acts of omission in denial of our ideals. But we have not boasted of our sins and have taken no pride in the injustices we have done. Where we have fallen short of our own belief, we have, when the fact has caught up with us, made public confession of our shortcomings and put on sackcloth and ashes for the whole world to see. A bad conscience is a peculiarly American national trait. Our failures have loomed large in the public eye, just because we have known in our hearts that the evil charged against us ran against our own beliefs as well as against our public protestations. In fact, we advertise our own failings to the world. It is almost a species of national self-flagellation. We will give a single case of denial of justice world-wide publicity because we know that it ought not to occur, and we are ashamed when it does.

But he who would understand the American role in the world must not confuse our failings with our commitments. These implicit attitudes are very real to us, and, quite unconsciously, we project them across our frontiers. We would build our relations with other nations on the beliefs by which we live. We cannot, in fact, do otherwise.

President Wilson expressed this idea in his Mobile address on October 27, 1913, by saying, "[Our] relationship with the rest of America is . . . [one] of a family of mankind, devoted to the development of true constitutional liberty." And "We should prove ourselves untrue to our own traditions if we proved ourselves untrue friends to them."[10]   [10] 63 Cong., 1 sess., *Sen. Doc. 226.*

29

The stream of that tradition is reflected in our belief that the individual is endowed with fundamental rights that are anterior to the existence of any government; that government rests upon the consent of the governed; that it is organized by them to serve their own best interests; that it has only a limited sovereignty because it is confined within a constitution which must respect the fundamental rights of the individual. These rights the individual cannot surrender, even if he wants to. That makes the state a corporation with limited powers. The federal system, in its turn, is a corporation composed of indestructible states, equal to each other. The federal government operates under a constitution with specifically prescribed powers, surrendered by the states for their own mutual benefit.

In our tradition, therefore, the individual is anterior to the state, and the state is anterior to the federal government. In the American conception, democracy rests upon individuals equal to each other, while the local, state, and federal governments are limited corporations, confined to the exercise of restricted powers prescribed by their respective constitutions. Neither the legislative nor the executive enjoys absolute sovereignty, and the judiciary is confined to keeping both within their constitutional limits. The projection of America abroad is, therefore, described within the broad conception of a world containing individuals endowed with fundamental rights and of governments possessed of limited sovereignty, operating in states that are equal to each other.

No government, however, can, in its international relations, live only by an abstract doctrine. The contradictory demands of daily life make any philosophy inadequate. This is especially the case with the government of the United States, which has no clear, conscious philosophy. For our democratic system rests largely upon habit and attitudes, while the commitments we have spoken of are in the background as a kind of censor, operating beneath the conscious level. But, if the commitments have not been reduced to a formal doctrine, they have not, for that reason, remained inoperative. On the contrary, they have come to the surface and influenced our final decisions in every important international crisis. Our policy, to be consistent with the ideals of the American people, must be anti-imperialist. It has to prove itself such even when, by transgressing American beliefs, it has taken a step in the direction of colonialism.

This is illustrated in the story of our relations with the Philippines. In the instructions issued by the President of the United States to the Commission for taking over the civil government of the Philippines from the military authorities, there were included the following collation of what was described as "certain great principles of government . . . which we deem essential to the rule of law, and the maintenance of individual freedom." These constitutional principles are spoken of as "rules of government," and are described as "inviolable."

"That no person shall be deprived of life, liberty or property, without due process of law; that private property shall not be taken for public use without just compensation; that in all criminal prosecutions the accused shall enjoy the right to a speedy and public trial, to be informed of the nature and cause of the accusation, to be confronted with the witnesses against him, to have compulsory process for obtaining witnesses in his favor, and to have the assistance of counsel for his defense; that excessive bail shall not be required, nor excessive fines imposed, nor cruel or unusual punishment inflicted; that no person shall be put twice in jeopardy for the same offense, or be compelled in any criminal case to be a witness against himself; that the right to be secure against unreasonable searches and seizures shall not be violated; that neither slavery nor involuntary servitude shall exist except as a punishment for crime; that no bill of attainder or *ex post facto* law shall be passed; that no law shall be passed abridging the freedom of speech or of the press or the rights of the people to peaceably assemble and petition the government for a redress of grievances; that no law shall be made respecting an establishment of religion or prohibiting the free exercise and enjoyment of religious profession and worship without discrimination or preference shall forever be allowed."[11]

The Supreme Court has described this collation of constitutional provisions in the following words:

"These words are not strange to the American lawyer or to the student of Constitutional history. They are in the familiar language of the Bill of Rights, slightly changed in form, as found in the nine amendments to the Constitution of the United States, with the omission of the provision preserving the right of trial by jury and the right of the people to bear arms, and adding the prohibition of the thirteenth amendment against slavery or involuntary servitude except as a punishment for crime, and that of Art. 1, par. 9, to the passage of bills of attainder and *ex post facto* laws. These principles ... were carefully collated from our own Constitution and embody almost verbatim the safeguards of that instrument for the protection of life and liberty."[12]

To this body of rights collated for the use of the Philippine Commission, the Supreme Court has attached the name of "fundamental rights."[13]

[11] *Kepner* v. *United States,* 195 U.S. 100, 123.
[12] *Ibid.,* 122, 123.

Furthermore, the Supreme Court has laid it down that there are "certain fundamental rights, recognized and declared, but not granted or created by the Constitution, and thereby guaranteed against violation or infringement by the United States, or by the States as the case may be."[14]

American imperialism and colonialism is thus circumscribed within these "fundamental rights," which it may not violate nor deny. But the recognition of these rights defeats, in the end, any imperial or colonial policy.

The acceptance of these "fundamental rights," "destroys all motive for conquest, since the only effect of conquest by us is to place upon us the difficult task of securing the fundamental rights of the individual in the countries annexed."[15]

The maintenance of these rights must result in the end either in the incorporation of the area as a state of the Union or in its independence. In the first instance, it would make the conquered area equal to each of the other states and a full participant in governing all the others. In the second, as in the case of the Philippines, the conquest would prove self-defeating.[16]

It should be noted further that the distinction drawn by the Supreme Court between incorporated and unin-

[13] *Ibid.*, 123, 199. *Hawaii* v. *Manchichi*, 190 U.S. 197, 217; *Dorr* v. *United States*, 195 U.S. 138, 144, 148.

[14] *Logem* v. *United States*, 144 U.S. 263, 293.

[15] Alpheus Henry Snow, "The American Philosophy of Government and Its Effect on International Relations," *The American Journal of International Law*, Vol. V (1914), 208–209.

[16] Puerto Rico is an interesting case of having all the practical benefit of full independence and most of those of complete membership in the federal system. It would stand to lose some valuable privileges if given full independence, or if it were incorporated as a state of the Union. Someone has described this as an instance of imperialism in reverse.

corporated territories did not affect the rule of "fundamental rights."[17] It did, however, make it easier to give
the Philippines their independence. If the Philippines
had been regarded as incorporated territory, then there
might have been constitutional difficulties in freeing the
islands.[18]

Clearly, the acceptance of the doctrine of "fundamental rights" makes it difficult for the United States to
become an imperial or colonial nation in the traditional
sense. More than that, our experience with Mexico suggests that these conceptions act as a barrier to our becoming an imperial nation in the more elusive and less responsible manner through the protection of foreign investments. For what the long and frequently bitter dispute with Mexico demonstrates is that, when it comes to
a final showdown, we will not use force and conquest in
defense of private investments. And, as we will not do
that, we cannot, in effect, "protect" the beneficiaries of
indirect imperialism.

The embodiment of the "fundamental rights" in our
constitutional system modifies for the United States the
traditional incentives of great powers in their relation
with weaker nations. This is true in spite of the Supreme
Court doctrine, in the so-called "Insular Cases," that the
Constitution does not follow the flag. For it is also part
of the same doctrine that the "fundamental rights" pre-
cede the flag. The Congress may, under the Constitution,
govern a territory, but only on condition that it maintains
the "fundamental rights." This, however, makes the
government of the territory a temporary tutelage or an
expensive and, in the end, an unworkable luxury. As
long as the American people adhere to their traditional

[17] *Dorr* v. *United States*, 195 U.S. 138.

[18] Julius W. Pratt, *American Colonial Experiment* (New York,
Prentice-Hall, 1950), 164.

beliefs, they cannot pursue the path of territorial or economic empire resting on force.

We have denied ourselves, unwittingly perhaps, but nonetheless effectively, the inducement that impelled a Roman, Spanish, British, French, German, and Russian Empire. The "American Century," whatever it may mean, does not mean an empire resting on force. It will be argued that such a position is purely negative, an elaboration of the strong isolationist tradition in the United States, and, whatever its abstract merits, not feasible in the present-day world.

In fact, the United States could not retire if it wanted to. The vacuum created by the destruction of the great powers of yesterday—Germany and Japan—and the weakening of Great Britain, France, and Italy, has to be filled, and, unless it is to be filled by Russia, it will have to be filled by the United States. We have, in fact, no choice in the matter. The American people cannot shrink from the world-wide role that destiny has cast for it. It can, however, only enter upon this perilous and unforeseen task in a manner consistent with its own experience and in consonance with its own ideals. The sudden demand upon American leadership was not of our making, but the conditions under which we will exercise the responsibilities thrust upon us can only be our own.

The key to our future role in the world is to be found in the things we did and tried to do in the past. Certainly since the First World War, and even before that, the American people have given strong evidence of a mighty penchant for some kind of world organization. It could almost be said that the American people have either sought to escape from the world or to organize it on some sort of a co-operative basis. Both of these motives have been active. If isolation is impossible—as it is—then world-wide co-operation is the only alternative policy that has evoked continuing interest.

Examples of this impelling concern are to be seen in the promotion of the World Court, the League to Enforce Peace, the Pan-American system, the League of Nations, and more recently, the United Nations. This persistent penchant for some kind of world order has to be explained because it is clear that American action, unless it is utterly defeated, will take that form, and can probably take no other. The only obvious and immediate answer to this puzzle lies in our belief in and experience with federalism as a system of government. When we think of permanent and workable relations between states, we automatically fall back upon our own federal experience.

But American federalism has certain special features that give it a peculiar significance in the modern world. For one thing, American federalism rests upon the accepted equality of states—the co-ordinate position of each state in the federal Union. There are no great and no small states in the American federal system. It rests upon the constitutional proviso that the federal government is only possessed of delegated powers, that no state can be divided or joined with another state without its own consent, and that no state can be deprived of its equal vote in the Senate without its own consent. The federal system is therefore an "indestructible union," resting upon "indestructible states."

Finally, the federal government and the states are possessed of only limited sovereignty, the first against the states, and both against the individual, who possesses "fundamental rights" which cannot be denied him and which he himself cannot surrender even if he wishes to. Incapacitated for traditional imperial expansion by its own commitments, as well as by its history and experience, the United States has turned to international organization resting upon a system of co-ordinate states as the only alternative to isolation. If it is going to play an active role in the world, it will attempt to project some such co-operative order among other nations. It is within that range of ideas and policies that American leadership can be expected to manifest itself, for the American people have, from the beginning, lived and worked with these ideas as a basis of co-operation between states.

The Co-ordinate State
as the Basis of American Federation

THE United States is the oldest international society (excepting Switzerland) in existence. It is also the largest. It is composed of forty-eight "indestructible," "sovereign" states, differing greatly in wealth and population. A comparison between Rhode Island and Texas in area, and between Nevada, with fewer than two hundred thousand in population, and New York, with over fourteen million, illustrates the point. And yet there is no invidious distinction between the states. Senator William Borah from a small state could be a powerful voice in the foreign policy of the United States for many years. In the United States, the representative of the smallest member of the federation can speak for the whole without anyone noting that he comes from the least of the states. This striking political achievement resulted from our acceptance of the principle of the juridical and political equality of the states. Without it, no nation based upon a federal system could have been built to span an entire continent and grow to be not merely the most powerful but also the stablest political entity on the face of the earth.

The issue of juridical and political equality of the states had to be settled first in the history of the United

States, or this nation might never have been born. This question was raised with the first movements towards political unification among the colonies. The colonies met as equals in the Stamp Act Congress of 1765. When the First Continental Congress assembled in 1774, the equal vote of the smaller colonies was challenged by the larger ones. Patrick Henry, in spite of declaring that the distinctions between Virginians, Pennsylvanians, New Yorkers, and New Englanders ". . . are no more, I am not a Virginian, I am an American,"[1] insisted that "it would be a great injustice if a little colony should have the same weight of a great one." He was supported by his colleague from Virginia, Benjamin Harrison, who said that if the small colonies were insistent upon their claims to equality, then he was "very apprehensive . . . we should not see them [the large states] at another convention."[2] But the crisis which had brought them together would not wait upon a full debate over what could, at the moment, be taken as a secondary question. The smaller colonies had their way, and the rule of the equal vote prevailed.

In 1776, when the Second Continental Congress gathered to deal with the burning issues of war and independence, the smaller colonies held stubbornly to the ideas which they had previously expressed. Witherspoon, the learned head of Princeton, who was one of the representatives of New Jersey, declared that "if an equal vote is refused, the smaller states will become vassals to the larger,"[3] and was answered by John Adams

[1] *Works of John Adams*, ed. by Charles Adams (Boston, Little, Brown and Co., 1850–56), II, 265–68. Quoted in Von Holst, *Constitutional History of the United States* (4 vols., Chicago, Callaghan and Co., 1877), I, 9–10.

[2] Edmund Cody Burnett, *The Continental Congress* (New York, Macmillan and Co., 1941), 37.

[3] *Ibid.*, 223.

from Massachusetts, "that an equal vote will endanger the larger states."[4]

Stephen Hopkins from Rhode Island showed that if the vote in the government was based upon population, the four large states would govern the nine smaller ones. In reply to the suggestion that under a confederation the older political differences were of little import, he said prophetically, "the safety of the whole depends upon the distinction of the colonies." This particularism is reflected in the remark by Major Sullivan that "a little colony has its all at stake as well as a great one."

The debate on the Articles of Confederation went on, with intermissions, from July, 1776, to November, 1777, but the ratification of the document they submitted to the local legislatures was only accomplished in 1781. The result was "a firm league of friendship," in which: "Each State retains its sovereignty, freedom and independence, and every power, jurisdiction and right, which is not by this Confederation expressly delegated to the United States, in Congress assembled." (Article II). With the Declaration of Independence, each state assumed for itself complete sovereignty. The states of Maryland, North Carolina, Massachusetts, and New Hampshire, among others, declared in their constitutions that sovereign power had again reverted to the people. So far as "legal theory is concerned, the case for state sovereignty seems complete."[5]

The Continental Congress was, therefore, an assemblage of diplomatic representatives. As an international diplomatic assembly, it had no powers of enforcement and possessed no independent income. It had to beg its

[4] *Ibid.*, 224.

[5] Evarts Boutell Greene, *The Foundations of American Nationality* (3 vols., New York, American Book Co., 1922), III, 558.

"requisition" from the states, had no machinery for implementing its laws, and no control over its own members, who could at any time be recalled by their respective governments.

Thomas Jefferson held that, once the purpose of the alliance (defense against British aggression) had been accomplished, the bond that brought the Continental Congress together ". . . was to expire of itself, and each state to become sovereign and independent in all things."[6]

The feeble Continental Congress was little heeded after the peace which recognized the independence of the United States. Differences between the states multiplied, and some of them proved too weak to maintain internal order. The Constitutional Convention, which gathered in Philadelphia on May 25, 1787, was designed to find some remedy to these difficulties and brought together many of the wisest and most experienced leaders of the day. Assembled for the purpose of reforming the Articles of Confederation, it turned instead to the drafting of a new constitution. The delegates represented sovereign political entities, and, as in the Continental Congress, each state enjoyed an equal vote.

James Brown Scott points out that ". . . it was an international convention or conference, in that it was composed of official representatives of twelve of the thirteen 'sovereign, free and independent' states of America, acting under instructions and meeting 'for the sole and express purpose of revising the Articles of Confederation' in order to 'render the federal constitution adequate to the exigencies of government, and the preservation of the union.' "[7]

[6] Von Holst, *Constitutional History*, I, 7 n.

[7] James Madison, *Debates in the Federal Convention of 1787 Which Framed the Constitution of the United States*, ed. by Gaillard Hunt and James Brown Scott (New York, G. P. Putnam's Sons, 1920).

How self-evident this seemed at the time is suggested by the remarks made on June 16, 1787, by Mr. William Paterson of New Jersey, ". . . all the states stand on a footing of equal sovereignty. . . . This is in the nature of all treaties."[8] But the difficulty lay just here. The Convention had been called together to find a way to a more effective government than had proven possible under the existing Confederation. The Constitutional Convention would have to find an acceptable compromise to the insistence of the small for equal powers with the large states, and the determination of the large states that equal voting rights in the government should be denied to the smaller ones. In fact, an effort to deny the smaller states their claim to equality began before the majority of the delegates had gathered at Philadelphia because it was argued that a good system of government ". . . could only be founded upon a denial of the claims of the smaller states."[9]

On the twenty-ninth of May, Edmund Randolph from Virginia proposed that representation in the national legislature ought to be "proportioned to the quotas of contribution, or to the numbers of free inhabitants."[10] Discussion on this proposal had to be postponed because the delegates from Delaware were restrained by their instruction from agreeing to any form other than that of an equal vote by each state.[11] The alternative was the possible withdrawal of the delegates from Delaware, and the threatened secession of a state within the first days of the meeting of the Constitutional Convention was fraught with grave danger. Other states might have followed Delaware and disrupted the gathering before it had settled down to its task. The dispute over represen-

[8] *Ibid.*, 105–106.   [9] *Ibid.*, n. 19.
[10] *Ibid.*, 23.   [11] *Ibid.*, 30.

tation remained a continuing threat to the Confederation until the final compromise between the larger and smaller states was agreed upon.

A way out of the difficulty was proposed early in the debate, on June 2, by John Dickinson from Delaware. The states would, he hoped, ". . . retain an equal voice at least in one house of the National Legislature."[12]

But this question had to be argued to the verge of dissolution before the proposal could be accepted. The bigger states pleaded their case on grounds of justice as well as interest. They had a greater population, a larger amount of property, and their weight in the government ought to be proportional. It was just that the majority of the people should control the government, and inexpedient that the richer states should be governed by the poorer ones. Some of the delegates were prepared to see the smaller states disappear altogether, and Gouverneur Morris from Pennsylvania said that if the smaller states would not unite on a just basis, unity would, in the end, be achieved by the sword, and Nathaniel Gorham from Massachusetts proposed that Delaware be added to Pennsylvania, and New Jersey divided between New York and Pennsylvania.[13]

James Wilson from Pennsylvania believed that state boundaries ought to be disregarded in elections to the Senate, and that districts consisting of smaller states and parts of larger ones should be laid out for that purpose.[14] Pinkney from South Carolina would have found a solution to the difficulty by grouping the states into different categories, entitled to three, two, and one votes respectively.[15] Alexander Hamilton argued that any system other than proportional representation would break down because "It is not in human nature that Virginia and other

[12] *Ibid.*, 48.   [13] *Ibid.*, 210.   [14] *Ibid.*, 72.   [15] *Ibid.*, 24.

large states should consent to it [equal suffrage], or if they did that they should long abide by it."[16]

In the face of the insistent demand for proportional representation as the only feasible basis for the future government of the United States, Brearly from New Jersey proposed that all the states be lumped together, and the map redrawn into thirteen equal parts, so that each state would then have an equal vote.[17] But this idea found no favor among the representatives of the large states. Wilson thought the plan totally impractical, and Madison noted that "the dissimilarities existing in the rules of property as well as in manners, habits and prejudices of the different states amounted to a prohibition of the attempt."[18] Madison, in spite of strongly urging the claims of the large states because "he did not conceive any effectual system could be substituted on any basis other than that of proportional suffrage,"[19] recognized the intrinsic merit of the independent states within the union and said that "he would preserve state rights, as carefully as trial by jury." But no amount of argument would move the little states from their position. They would either have an equal vote with the larger ones or see the Confederation break up. To Wilson's implied threat that the large states would never agree to equality and would federate among themselves, Paterson replied, "Let them do it. But they have no authority to compel others to unite. New Jersey would never agree. She would be swallowed up. He had rather submit to a monarch, to a despot, than to such a fate."[20]

How close the issue had now been drawn is shown in the remarks of Gunning Bedford from Delaware: "The large states dare not dissolve the confederation.

[16] *Ibid.*, 114.   [17] *Ibid.*, 80–81.   [18] *Ibid.*, 12.
[19] *Ibid.*, 98.   [20] *Ibid.*, 82.

If they do, the small states will find some foreign ally of more honor and good faith who will take them by the hand and do them justice."[21]

The grounds on which the small states made their case are revealing, for they implied the reason for the success of the American federal system. The states, Martin from Maryland said, being equal, cannot give up an equality of votes without giving up their liberty. Virginia, Massachusetts, and Pennsylvania "would have 42/90 of the votes." They could do as they pleased "without a miraculous union of the other ten." Greater power for the large states would lead to alliances among the states for self-defense. According to Bedford, in the proposed legislature Delaware would have one-ninetieth of the vote, while Pennsylvania and Virginia would have one-third of the whole. It seemed to him that the delegates from the large states wished "for . . . monstrous influence."[22]

Brearly made clear what would, in the light of past experience, have been the likely result if the large states had succeeded in forcing their views upon the Constitutional Convention. "If proportional representation prevailed, Virginia would have 16 votes, Georgia one. There will be three large states and ten small ones. Massachusetts, Pennsylvania and Virginia will carry everything before them. *There would be danger of combination. Georgia with her solitary vote, and the other little states will be obliged to throw themselves constantly into the scale of some larger one in order to have any weight at all.*"[23] [author's italics.] That is, it would lead to the establishment of a system of balance of power between the states, and as William Paterson implied, to aggrandizement. "Give the larger States an influence in proportion

[21] *Ibid.*, 199.   [22] *Ibid.*, 78.   [23] *Ibid.*, 80–81.

to their magnitude, and what will be the consequence? Their ambition will be proportionally increased, and the small State will have everything to lose."[24] Therefore, in the view of the leaders of the small states, the preservation of the federal system, the avoidance of combinations between states for purposes of achieving a balance of power among themselves, and the escape of the consequent dangers of conspiring by the states against each other depended upon the acceptance of the co-ordinate position of each state in the proposed union.

The only solution acceptable to the small states was the compromise on proportional representation in the House of Representatives and an equal vote in the Senate. This proposal was made by the delegates from Connecticut, William Samuel Johnson, Roger Sherman, and Oliver Ellsworth: "Everything depended upon this. The smaller States would never agree to the plan on any other principle than an equality of suffrage in this branch."[25] Ellsworth added, "If all the States are to exist, they must of necessity have an equal vote in the general government. Small communities, when associating with greater, can only be supported by an equality of votes."[26] Unless the larger states were prepared to accept this principle, "We will be forever separated. . . ." The question was brought to a head by Martin, who declared that "you must give all States an equal suffrage, or our business is at an end."[27]

To avoid imminent dissolution of the Convention, and the greater danger that the Confederation of the American States would break up, a committee was appointed to seek some way out of the dilemma. In its report, the

[24] *Ibid.*, 82.

[25] *Ibid.*, 88–89.

[26] *United States. Formation of the Union;* Documents, arranged by Charles C. Tansill (Library of Congress, Washington, D. C., 1927), 827.

[27] *Ibid.*, 837.

committee upheld the view of the smaller states, but as before, the larger states found the proposal unacceptable, and the vote on the committee's report was a tie.

A young delegate from Georgia, Abraham Baldwin, broke the impasse by changing his vote in favor of the smaller states. He had been born in Connecticut, had taught at Yale, and then removed to Georgia. In commenting upon this compromise, John Fiske has drawn attention to the long federal history of Connecticut. The Hartford Convention of 1639 brought together the towns of Windsor, Hartford, and Westerfield upon a basis of equality. It also adopted the first written American constitution. This gave the towns an equal vote in the General Court. In the election of governor, however, the rule of a simple majority was followed. It also conferred upon the General Court only such powers as were expressly granted. When the debates in the Constitutional Convention had reached a climax, the three delegates from Connecticut proposed, as a way out of the seemingly insoluble difficulty, the adoption of the system long in existence in Connecticut. They proposed, as we have seen, an equal vote for the states in the Senate and representation according to population in the House. This gave the larger states a majority in the one, and the smaller states in the other. Benjamin Franklin, who was one of the Pennsylvania delegation, saw the reasonableness of this suggestion and favored its acceptance. But the larger states held their old ground and voted against the committee report. The argument of the smaller states prevailed with the support, as we mentioned above, of the delegate from Georgia who had lived under the Connecticut system before removing to the South.[28]

[28] John Fiske, *Essays, Historical and Literary* (2 vols., New York, The Macmillan Co., 1902), II, 123-61.

It was thus that the principle of the co-ordinate state became the basis upon which the United States was to be established. In effect, this means that the smaller states can outvote the larger ones in the Senate, and that in any crucial legislative issue the states are equal because a bill has to be passed by both houses. It also means that in foreign relations the smaller states could play the decisive role if they voted as states. But they do not vote that way. As so clearly foreseen by Paterson and Brearly, equality eliminated the dangers of alliance among the states.

The acceptance of the principle of the co-ordinate state has produced a unique political structure, a federal system composed of equally sovereign states, combined for purposes of more effective government. But the Union has not destroyed the state. In fact, the state has remained the basis of the nation and of the national government. This was clearly foreseen by the founding fathers. The long and bitter debate over the adoption of the Constitution hinged largely on this issue. The opponents of the new instrument of national government, like Patrick Henry and Martin, feared that it would destroy the states and, by destroying them, open the road to tyranny. Those who fought for the adoption of the Constitution argued with great vigor and conviction that the preservation of the state was essential to the preservation of the Union, and that the states could not be destroyed by the federal government because it rested upon them. Alexander Hamilton, always cited as the most insistent nationalist, said in defense of the Constitution: "The gentlemen are afraid that the state governments will be abolished. But, sir, their existence does not depend upon the laws of the United States. Congress can no more abolish the state governments, than they can dissolve the Union."[29] He added, "The states can never lose their powers till the whole people of America are robbed of their liberties. These must go together; they must support each other, or meet one common fate."[30]

This defense of the Constitution as resting upon the co-ordinate position of the state is repeated over and over again. Mr. Oliver Wolcott from Connecticut argued that "The Constitution effectually secures the states in their several rights. It must secure them for its own sake; for they are the pillars which uphold the general system."[31] And to cite only one more bit of evidence of the insistence by those who urged the adoption of the Constitution that the preservation of the states was essential to the survival of the Union itself, we will quote Davie from North Carolina: "The Federal Convention were as well convinced as the members of this house, that the state governments were absolutely necessary to the existence of the federal government. They considered them as the great massy pillars on which this political fabric was to be extended, and supported; and were fully persuaded that, when they were removed, or should moulder down by time, the general government must tumble into ruin. . . ."[32]

We have emphasized this point because it is crucial not merely to an understanding of the nature of American federalism, but defines the conception of the co-ordinate state that has governed our attitude towards the nations beyond our borders. The national government rests upon the states, and is dependent upon them. We tend to forget this because we take it so much for granted. It is worth reproducing James Bryce's comments upon

[29] Elliot, *Debates on the Constitution*, II, 319.
[30] *Ibid.*, 355.   [31] *Ibid.*, 202.
[32] *Ibid.*, IV, 58.

this question. He saw it so clearly, partly because he could look at it from the outside.

"America is a commonwealth of commonwealths, a Republic of Republics, a State which, while one, is never the less composed of other states even more essential to its existence than it is to theirs. . . ."

"The States, are [not] mere subdivisions of the Union, never creatures of the national government, like the counties of England or the departments of France. . . . They have not been called into being by that government. They existed before. They could exist without it."[33]

". . . The American States are now all inside the Union, and have all become subordinate to it. Yet the Union is more than an aggregate of States, and the States are more than parts of the union. It might be destroyed, and they, by adding a few further attributes of power to those they now possess, might survive as independent, self-governing communities."[34]

We are not conscious of being an international society because we do not quarrel about the equal right to partake in a common decision. We tend to overlook the fact that we are a federation of many political entities, differing greatly in size, population, and social mores, because the difference in size and wealth among the states has little perceptible influence upon the internal or external policies of the nation.

Political pluralism has given the United States its vigor and vitality as well as its stability. Dickinson was speaking with the deepest political insight when he said, "One source of stability is the double branch of the legislature. The division of the country into distinct states

---

[33] James Bryce, *The American Commonwealth* (2 vols., New York, The Macmillan Co., 1902), I, 13–14.
[34] *Ibid.*, II, 1.

formed the other principal source of stability."[35] "It will produce that collision between the different authorities which should be wished for in order to check each other."[36]

If these political arrangements prepared a federal union, the principles of the Northwest Ordinance assured its ultimate expansion to the Pacific. Next to the formation of the Union itself, the Northwest Ordinance represents the most important single political decision of the American people. The cession of the ill-defined and overlapping claims to western territorial lands was necessary to the establishment of the Union. But the decision to divide this vast area into separate states and admit them, each in turn, upon a footing of equality with the old states was not only something new in territorial policy but was an act of the highest political wisdom. For it is upon this decision that it has been possible to organize a continent into a single federation and have it last until it is now one of the oldest governments in the world, and the most stable. This act makes manifest the American commitment to the ideal of the co-ordinate state. There was danger, it was argued, in admitting this territory into the Union, and greater danger that the new states would outnumber the original thirteen that had won their independence and organized the government, and that the original states would one day be exposed to the power of states then not in existence. The new area could have been retained as a dependency, the states, if formed, could have been admitted as junior partners, as less worthy of the full membership won by so much sacrifice by the first partners of the Union. Both suggestions were made and repudiated. What prevailed was the ideal of the co-ordinate state.

[35] Elliot, *Debates on the Constitution*, 47.
[36] *Ibid.*, 72.

The draft of the Northwest Ordinance submitted by Thomas Jefferson in 1784 proposed that the states be carved out of the western lands and admitted on a footing of equality with those then in existence. A resolution by Theodoric Bland, seconded by Alexander Hamilton, provided that the new districts "should become and ever after be and constitute a separate, free and sovereign state, and be admitted into the union as such, with all the privileges and immunities of those states which now compose the union."[37] The final ordinance, as passed in 1787, substantially satisfied this principle, making a requirement for a democratic government and a population of sixty thousand.

When this question came before the Constitutional Convention, however, strong opposition developed to the principle of equality which the Continental Congress had laid down. Hugh Williamson from North Carolina feared the admission of the new states from the West because they would be small and ". . . would be tempted to combine to lay burdens on commerce and consumption. . . ."[38] Gouverneur Morris was more positive in his opposition. He feared the future loss of power by the original states. "Provision ought therefore be made to prevent the maritime states from being outvoted. This could be done by fixing irrevocably the representation which the Eastern States should have and the number to be allotted to each new state."[39] If they ever outnumbered the original states, they would ruin the Atlantic economy.

John Rutledge and Rufus King supported these arguments, and Pierce Butler pleaded for some balance of

[37] Burnett, *The Continental Congress*, 598.
[38] Elliot, *Debates on the Constitution*, 177.
[39] *Ibid.*, 212.

power between the old and the new states. Gorham argued that "... the Atlantic States, having the Government in their own hands, may take care of their own interest by dealing out the right of representation in safe proportions to the Western States."[40] Elbridge Gerry from Massachusetts made a motion, "That in order to secure the liberties of the States already confederated, the number of representatives in the first branch of the Congress of the States which shall hereafter be established, shall never exceed in number the representatives from such States as shall accede to this confederation."[41] The original thirteen states were to be protected forever against the future power of the new states.

It can be seen that a substantial part of the leading delegates from the larger states opposed the acceptance of the principle laid down by the Continental Congress when it adopted the Northwest Ordinance. But when it came to final settling of the issue, the principle of the co-ordinate character of the states prevailed here as it had in the struggles for the voting rights of the small states. Some of the arguments advanced in support of the provisions of the Northwest Ordinance deserve repetition here because they bear directly upon the governing conception in our foreign policy.

Madison, in dealing with the question of the western states, repeated the position he had taken in the Continental Congress when the matter was first under discussion. "... He was clear and firm in opinion, that no unfavorable distinctions were admissible, either in point of justice or policy."[42] Mason argued that the western states must "be treated as equals, and subjected to no degrading discriminations." He saw clearly that, unless the new

---

[40] *Ibid.*, 224.   [41] *Ibid.*, 251.
[42] *Ibid.*, 236.

states were given a co-ordinate position, the expansion of the United States to the West would be endangered and perhaps made impossible, for, "they will have the same pride and other passions which we have, and will either not unite with, or will speedily revert from the union, if they are not in all respects placed on an equal footing with their brethren."[43]

Randolph brought the question of the character of the democratic process into the discussion and agreed with Mason that a denial of equality to the new states would place the American government in jeopardy. He laid it down that "if a fair representation of the people be not secured, the injustice of the government will shake it to its foundations. Congress has pledged the public faith to the new states, that they shall be admitted on equal terms. They never would nor ought to accede on any other. . . ."[44]

Pinkney of Virginia had before argued that "conquest or superiority among other powers is not, or ought not ever to be the object of republican systems."[45] Robert Morris said that the people from the western states ought to be treated "with equality which will make them friends, not enemies." The ideal of the co-ordinate state prevailed for the western territories.

This same principle was later applied to the lands that came with the Louisiana Purchase. The treaty transferring that territory from France to the United States said in Article III: "The inhabitants of the ceded territory shall be incorporated in the union of the United States and admitted as soon as possible according to the principle of the Federal Constitution, to the enjoyment of all rights, advantages and immunities of citizens of the United States, and in the meantime they shall be

[43] *Ibid.*, 232.   [44] *Ibid.*, 233.   [45] *Ibid.*, 161.

maintained and protected in the free enjoyment of their liberty, property, and the religion which they profess."

This same doctrine was later written in the Transcontinental Treaty, negotiated by John Quincy Adams with Spain, and was further applied to the vast territory acquired by the United States as a result of the war with Mexico. The principle of the co-ordinate state was further evidenced by the constitutional proviso that no large state could be divided, and no small state united with another without its own consent. It was only on this basis that a continent could have been brought within a permanent federal system.

Daniel Webster does not overstate the case when he says, "I doubt whether one single law or any lawgiver, ancient or modern, has produced effects of more distinct, marked, and lasting character than the Ordinance of 1787."[46]

It should be noted that the Ordinance embodies a new principle governing the relation between colonies and the parent state. In the past colonies had continued in a subordinate position or become independent of the mother country. The Northwest Ordinance substituted the principle of union based upon equal sovereignty as the governing feature between older and younger states. The very concept of colony seems to be repugnant to the principle of the co-ordinate state.[47]

The juridical and political equality of the "indestructible" states has made possible sharp difference of opinion over questions of interest and policy without undermining the Union. *What we have not quarreled about is the right of each state to its full share in a common*

[46] Quoted by John Fiske, *The Critical Period in American History* (New York, Houghton Mifflin and Co., 1898), 206.

[47] Greene, *American Nationality*, 578.

judgment and in the formation of a common policy. And herein lies the basic issue in international relations.

The "fundamental principle" of co-ordinate membership within the federal Union ultimately eventuated in Calhoun's doctrine of a dissoluble compact between the states and in the Civil War. The South still speaks of the War Between the States. But this same principle also explains the even more remarkable political event of the readmission of the defeated on a par with the victorious states. If the Union was to survive, no other course was possible. A federal union built upon the principle of equal sovereignty is not a proper instrument for military government, nor for the arbitrary denial to others of the rights and immunities which the individual states claim for themselves. The American conception of co-ordinate states is, in its essence, anticolonial.

☆ 3 ☆

The Co-ordinate State
and the Monroe Doctrine

THE American people, as we saw in the last chapter, have been deeply influenced by the idea of the equal sovereignty of states. This concept justified their rebellion against Great Britain and shaped their territorial policy. It was also to prove the governing proposition in their foreign policy. The Monroe Doctrine, and nearly every other important foreign policy decision since then, has reflected this same basic political belief.

Two years before the Monroe Doctrine was given to the world, John Quincy Adams, whose firm hand shaped its final form, had declared that "colonial establishments [were] . . . incompatible with the essential character of our institutions," and that the time had arrived for them to "come to an end."[1] In announcing the new doctrine, our government chose to "act separately," rather than with Great Britain as originally proposed by Canning.

President Monroe consulted his two predecessors, Jefferson and Madison, on Canning's interesting suggestion. Jefferson approved the proposal to "protest against the atrocious violations of the rights of nations, so flagi-

[1] Samuel Flagg Bemis, *John Quincy Adams and the Foundations of American Foreign Policy* (New York, A. A. Knopf, 1949), 368.

tiously begun by Bonaparte, and now continued by the equally lawless Alliance, calling itself Holy . . . ," and went on to add he could honestly say that ". . . we aim not at the acquisition of any of those [former Spanish] possessions . . . that we will oppose, with all our means, the forcible interposition of any other power. . ."[2] while Madison would have broadened the declaration aimed at the Holy Alliance to embrace not only the Latin-American republics but Spain and Greece as well. President Monroe's declaration must, therefore, be read in the light of the anti-imperialism and anticolonialism of its chief American sponsors.

The Monroe Doctrine asserted the opposition of the United States to any further colonization by European governments in the Western Hemisphere, and to intervention in the affairs of the newly established republics. But John Quincy Adams and Henry Clay were prepared to broaden the doctrine from a unilateral to a multilateral policy, as well as to assert the principle of nonintervention by any nation in the affairs of another.

In his message urging United States participation in the Panama Congress, sent to the Senate on December 26, 1825, President John Quincy Adams proposed the desirability of "an agreement between all the parties that each will guard by its own means against the establishment of any future European colony within its borders."[3] He added, in words that have the ring of the "good neighbor" in them, that ". . . we have laid the foundation of our future intercourse with them in the broadest principles of reciprocity and the most cordial feelings of fraternal friendship . . . and to hand down that friendship to

[2] *The Writings of Thomas Jefferson,* ed. by H. A. Washington (9 vols., Washington, D. C., 1853–54), VII, 315–17.

[3] *Messages and Papers of the Presidents,* ed. by James D. Richardson (10 vols., Washington, D. C., Government Printing Office, 1896–1899), II, 319.

future ages is congenial to the highest policy of the union, as it will be to all those nations and their posterity."[4]

He returned to urge these same ideas on March 15, 1826, in his message to the House of Representatives, asking for the appropriation of funds for the United States delegates. If, on this occasion, he was more restrained in his statement, it was due to the bitter opposition that had arisen in the Senate. But the idea of a common policy with the Latin-American nations on the principles of the Monroe Doctrine is repeated: "Most of the new American republics," he said, have given their assent to the principles of the Monroe Doctrine, and ". . . a *joint* declaration of its character . . . may be . . . all that the occasion would require." [author's italics][5]

Clearly, John Quincy Adams, who had played so large a role in the development of the Monroe Doctrine, was prepared to universalize it among the nations of this hemisphere rather than to confine it within its unilateral character.

Henry Clay makes even more evident that, in its earliest days, the Monroe Doctrine was conceived as a hemispheric policy. In the instructions written out for the guidance of the United States plenipotentiaries, Clay, as secretary of state, speaks of treaties ". . . laying the foundation of lasting amity and good neighborhood."[6] He goes on to propose: ". . . a joint declaration of the several American States, each, however, acting for and binding only itself, that within the limits of their respective territories no new European colony will hereafter be allowed to be established."[7]

If, in the case of Cuba, Clay reaffirms the nontransfer

---

[4] *Ibid.*, 319–20.   [5] *Ibid.*, 235.

[6] Henry Clay's Instructions to United States Delegates, *International Conference*, IV. Historical Appendix (Washington, D. C., Government Printing Office, 1890), 123.

[7] *Ibid.*, 137.

principle and suggests that the United States would oppose its conquest by Mexico and Colombia, he also states
the conditions of and the preference for Cuban independence in words that reflect a philosophy of politics
peculiarly congenial to the American people. "If Cuba
had the ability . . . of maintaining an independent self-
government . . . we should prefer to see it in that state,
because we desire the happiness of others as well as ourselves, and we believe that is most likely to be secured
by a local government springing directly from, and identified in feeling, interest and sympathy with the people
to be governed."[8]

More important in its long range implications is his
statement of the principle of nonintervention, not only
by European nations, but by all nations. He would make
it clear to the delegates at the Panama Congress that the
United States, "allowing no interference," in their internal affairs, "are equally scrupulous in refraining from
all interference. . ." in the affairs "of other independent
nations." [author's italics][9] And "you will . . . inculcate
the solemn duty of every nation to reject *all* foreign dic-
tation in its domestic concerns. . . ." [author's italics] It
would be difficult to state the doctrine of nonintervention more tersely or with greater emphasis.

More than a century was to pass before these original
propositions of John Quincy Adams and Henry Clay
were to be brought forward again by Franklin Delano
Roosevelt, Cordell Hull, and Sumner Welles and made
the cornerstone of the Pan-American system. But it
would be wrong to assume that they were entirely for-
gotten. It is significant that the doctrine of nonintervention by European nations is never so stated (except in the
Roosevelt corollary) as to give the United States the

[8] *Ibid.*, 138.   [9] *Ibid.*, 148.

right to police American affairs. This point deserves emphasis. Opposition to European intervention was not taken as a warrant for the United States to break a general rule.

The Monroe Doctrine was little heard of between 1826 and 1848. In that year President Polk, in his first annual message, interpreted it to mean that "... the nations of America are equally sovereign and independent with those of Europe."[10]

But it was William H. Seward who spelled out the "fundamental principle" of the "co-ordinate state" whilst urging the French to withdraw their army from Mexico, and argued that intervention was incompatible with "sovereignty and independence."[11] "If one state has a right to intervene in any other, to establish discipline, constituting itself a judge of the occasion, then every state has the same right to intervene in the affairs of every other nation, being itself above the arbiter, both in regard to the time and the occasion. The principle of intervention, thus practically carried out, would seem to render all sovereignty and independence, and even all international peace and amity, uncertain and fallacious."

If this is a broad philosophical statement against the right of intervention by one state in the affairs of another, Seward accepts its implication for the conduct of the United States. The French, in yielding to the pressure of the United States for the withdrawal of their troops from Mexico, had subtly argued that if they were expected to accept the rule of nonintervention, then "... our honor, commands us to expect ... that the American people will themselves conform to the law which they invoke...." It was in answer to this note that Seward said:

[10] Richardson, *Messages and Papers*, IV, 398.

[11] 39 Cong., 1 sess., House Exec. Doc. (Serial no. 1261), No. 93, 589–98.

"The practice of this government, from the beginning, is a guarantee to all nations of the respect of the American people for the free sovereignty of the people in every other state. . . . It is in reality the chief element of foreign intercourse in our history."

The doctrine of nonintervention, therefore, is not something recent and new in the United States. It was not first asserted under the auspices of the Good Neighbor policy, and even the phrase of "good neighbor" itself is not new. It was used, as we have seen, by Clay, and during the Grant administration, it was used by Charles Sumner. What is new is the writing of this principle into a formal treaty. It may be true that the Monroe Doctrine, as has been argued, does not contain a self-denying ordinance. But in successive statements of the theory, it has been repeatedly asserted that the injunction against European colonization or intervention is not meant to facilitate our indulgence in practices we condemn in others.

In the statement of national policy towards Latin America, the diplomatic record of the United States reveals rare consistency. From the beginning we supported the proposition that the integrity of the independent American nations must be respected. Hamilton Fish, writing to President Grant, called attention to the fact that ". . . the duty of non-interference has been admitted by every president."[12]

President Grant, when speaking of Cuba, repeated this same idea. He expressed the hope that the European dependencies would, in time, become ". . . members of the family of nations . . . independent powers. . . ."[13]

[12] John Bassett Moore, *History and Digest of the International Arbitration to Which the United States Has Been a Party* (Washington, D. C., Government Printing Office, 1901), ix.

Surprisingly, perhaps, Richard Olney adhered to the same doctrine. He boasted in the Venezuelan dispute with Great Britain that a fiat of the United States "is law upon the subjects to which it confines its interposition" in this continent. But this does not keep him from saying that the Monroe Doctrine ". . . does not contemplate interference in the internal affairs of any American State."[14] He asserted, in words reminiscent of the great debate in the Constitutional Convention, here transferred to a debate between nations, that "the United States would cherish as its own the territorial rights of the feeblest of those states regarding them . . . as equal even to the greatest nationalities."

It was left to Theodore Roosevelt temporarily to twist the Monroe Doctrine beyond its historical intent. He argued that, "however reluctantly," the United States might be compelled "to the exercise of an international police power" in the Caribbean area. But even Roosevelt's exuberance was modulated by the basic American tradition. Theodore Roosevelt's name is so closely associated with the notion of the "big stick" in American foreign policy, and with the belief that the United States was bent upon an expanding imperialism, that it is worth noting that even he could not entirely escape the force of the idea that all states are co-ordinate, are of equal rank and dignity, and that intervention in, or the suppression of another state, no matter how small, runs counter to the American tradition.

We find, therefore, that Roosevelt, in his annual message to Congress in 1901, said, "The Monroe Doctrine should be the cardinal feature of the foreign policy of all the nations of the two Americas, as it is of the United

[13] Richardson, *Messages and Papers*, VII, 32.
[14] 54 Cong., 1 sess., *House Exec. Doc.* (Serial no. 3368), No. 1, 545–62.

States." This is essentially the view of John Quincy Adams and Henry Clay. But Roosevelt went further than that. He added that if it opposes foreign territorial conquest in this hemisphere, it is not ". . . intended to give cover to any aggression by a New World power at the expense of any other."[15] He specifically says, "We have not the slightest desire to secure any territory at the expense of our neighbors."[16] In his second annual message he said, "No independent nation in America need have the slightest fear of aggression from the United States."[17]

It was in 1904 that he expanded the Doctrine by adding what has become known as the "Roosevelt corollary" to justify intervention in the Caribbean countries in the case of "chronic wrongdoing, or an impotence which results in a general loosening of the ties of civilized society."[18] He is not arguing for the right of conquest by the United States, nor even for the right of permanent intervention. "If all of the republics to the south of us will only grow" stable, orderly, and prosperous, "all need for us to be the special champion of the Doctrine will disappear. Under no circumstances will the United States use the Monroe Doctrine as a cloak for territorial oppression."[19]

The violent criticism, both in the United States and in Latin America, of the new slant given to the Doctrine by Theodore Roosevelt evoked something like an apologetic response from the author of the corollary. He denies that the corollary carried with it a right to a protectorate over our weaker neighbors. "Nothing could be

[15] *Foreign Relations of the United States* (Washington, D. C., Government Printing Office, 1901), *ix.*

[16] *Ibid.*

[17] *Foreign Relations,* 1902, *ix.*

[18] 58 Cong., 3 sess., *House Doc.* (Serial no. 4780), No. 1, *xli–ii.*

[19] *Foreign Relations,* 1905, *ix–xxxiii.*

farther from the truth."[20]The Roosevelt administration
is not sufficient evidence that the older tradition was completely abandoned. It was while the author of the "corollary" to the Monroe Doctrine occupied the White House
that Elihu Root, his secretary of state, made the ever
memorable statement of America's attitude to Latin
America in an address delivered at Rio de Janeiro, during a meeting of the Third International Conference of
American States in July, 1906: "We deem the independence and equal rights of the smallest and weakest member of the family of nations entitled to as much respect
as those of the greatest empire. . . . We neither claim nor
desire any rights or privileges or powers that we do not
freely concede to every American Republic."[21] This eloquent statement has enriched the language with which the
American tradition of the co-ordinate state is described.

Within a few years President Woodrow Wilson was
to elaborate upon these same ideas in words that attracted
the attention of the world. He made more evident the
route we have, in fact, always followed. "The United
States has nothing to seek in central and South America
except the lasting interests of the peoples of the two con-
tinents."[22] Later in the same year, at Mobile, on October
27, he told his audience: "You cannot be friends upon
any other terms than upon terms of equality. . . . The
United States will never again seek one additional foot
of territory by conquest . . . our real relationship with the
rest of America is [that] of a family of mankind. . ."[23]

[20] *Ibid.*, 1906, *vii–xiv.*

[21] Robert Bacon and James Brown Scott, *Latin America and the
United States: Addresses by Elihu Root* (Cambridge, Harvard University
Press, 1917), 6.

[22] *Foreign Relations*, 1913, 7.

[23] *The New Democracy: Presidential Messages, Addresses and Other
Papers (1913–1917) by Woodrow Wilson (Published Papers of Wood-*

These statements are striking and eloquent, but their real significance lies in Wilson's knowing that "we should prove ourselves untrue to our own traditions if we prove ourselves untrue friends to them. . . ."[24]

Wilson understood, even if in the war years he did not always act upon this knowledge in relation to the weaker countries of the Caribbean, that American foreign relations were an unconscious projection to the outside world of the basic American tradition of the co-ordinate state. That is why he could speak with such confidence, and that is why he had such wide support among the American people. In 1915, Wilson proposed the formalization of the idea of co-ordinate membership in this hemisphere by a treaty which would guarantee the territorial integrity and political independence of the American nations, so that, to use Colonel House's words, "The Monroe Doctrine may be upheld by all the American Republics instead of by the United States alone as now."[25]

If Charles Evans Hughes is less eloquent than Wilson, he is no less clear about the controlling proposition in American foreign relations. Like Wilson, he falls back upon the basic tradition of the people of the United States. "Anyone who really understands our people must realize that the last thing in the world we desire is to assume responsibility as to other peoples. . . ."[26] And he, like former secretaries of state, expresses the hope that ". . . the [Monroe] doctrine would have the support of all American Republics," and repeats the idea that "the Pan American Union is based on the principle of the equality of the American States."[27]

row *Wilson*, 6 vols., III–IV, ed. by Ray Stannard Baker and William E. Dodd (New York, Harper and Bros., 1926), 67.

[24] *Ibid.*, 69.

[25] Department of State, *The Lansing Papers*, II, 486.

[26] Charles Evans Hughes,*The Pathway of Peace* (New York, Harper and Bros., 1925), 164.

The continuing criticism of the Roosevelt corollary, both in the United States and in Latin America, and the persistent opposition to the intervention of the United States in the Caribbean countries led to an official review of the meaning of the Monroe Doctrine. At the suggestion of President Herbert Hoover, J. Reuben Clark, the undersecretary of state, undertook to prepare a memorandum on the Doctrine in 1928. This document, which was published by the Department of State in 1930, officially repudiates the Roosevelt corollary, and brings the policy back to its original purpose. It restates the proposition that the Monroe Doctrine is aimed at the protection of the Latin-American countries against the threat of intervention and colonization from Europe, that it does not give any warrant for United States intervention in Latin America, and says specifically that the Roosevelt corollary cannot be derived from the Monroe Doctrine. "The so-called Roosevelt corollary . . . is . . . not justified by the terms of the Monroe Doctrine. . . . So far as Latin America is concerned, the Doctrine is now, and has always been, not an instrument of violence and aggression, but an unbought, freely bestowed, and wholly effective guaranty of their freedom, independence, and territorial integrity against the imperialistic designs of Europe."[28]

The Good Neighbor policy is therefore the logical sequence to a tradition as old as our government, and was foreshadowed in the words and policies of John Quincy Adams and Henry Clay. The crystallization of the ideas expressed in connection with the Panama Congress of 1826 had to wait upon the cumulative impacts

[27] *Ibid.*
[28] J. Reuben Clark, "Memorandum on the Monroe Doctrine," Publication No. 37, Department of State, 1930.

of a century-long history and the dramatic events of the
Second World War before they could be written into
treaties embodying a system of collective security for the
Western Hemisphere. Secretary of State Cordell Hull's
definition of the co-ordinate position of the American
States as consisting of "the absolute independence, the
unimpaired sovereignty, the perfect equality, and the
political integrity of each nation large and small. . ." has
a classic finality about it.[29]

The Nonintervention Doctrine enunciated by Franklin D. Roosevelt in 1933 (Department of State, Press
Release, December 30, 1933), the series of resolutions
beginning with the Havana Conference in 1940 and cul-
minating in the Rio de Janeiro Treaty of 1947, and the
charter of the Organization of American States signed at
the Bogota Conference in 1948, converted the Monroe
Doctrine from a unilateral to a multilateral policy. Wilson's hope, embodied in the proposed treaty of 1915, had
been fulfilled.

Bolivar's effort of 1826 to form a federation of American nations was resuscitated by James G. Blaine when he
called together a Pan-American Congress in Washington
in 1889. Eighteen American nations gathered in response
to the call, and in making the opening address, Blaine
repeats once again what almost every American states-
man has said about these nations. "[They] . . . shall . . .
meet on terms of absolute equality . . ." and in a spirit
that will ". . . tolerate no spirit of conquest." In the sixty-
three years of its existence, this organization has gradually grown in prestige, influence, and vitality. The
treaties and conventions agreed upon have grown in im-

[29] *Report of the Delegates of the United States of America to the
Seventh International Conference of American States* (Washington, D. C.,
Government Printing Office, 1934), 114.

portance, and since the Montevideo meeting of 1936, it has, by the gradual accretion of new treaties, become the instrument of collective security in the Western Hemisphere. The plans projected at the Panama Congress of 1826 have at last come to fruition. The treaties that have grown out of the Inter-American conferences since 1936 have given legal substance to the idea of the co-ordinate state. They have formalized the principles of nonintervention and territorial integrity. They have also converted the Monroe Doctrine from a unilateral declaration to a multilateral policy, and have established in Inter-American law both the doctrine and the machinery for the enforcement of collective security against external as well as against aggression from within the American Hemisphere.

This has only been possible because the states met and worked together as equals. The principle of the co-ordinate state, incorporated into the constitutional system of the United States and projected for the rest of the hemisphere by John Quincy Adams and Henry Clay, has now been extended to the hemisphere. As President Franklin D. Roosevelt remarked in 1940, "We of this Hemisphere have no need to seek a new international order, we have already found it."[30]

[30] Department of State *Bulletin*, Vol. II, No. 43, p. 403.

4

The Co-ordinate State
and Latin America

THE Monroe Doctrine we reviewed in the last chapter is often stated in lofty and ideal terms. It recalls John Quincy Adams' oration on the Fourth of July, 1821, when he asserted that the Declaration of Independence had "destroyed all rights of conquest." It is consistent with the theme argued in the Constitutional Convention that a democratic government could not be imperialist. This is the theoretical view. Practical policy, however, has more than once contradicted the declared doctrine. The war with Mexico and the repeated interventions in the West Indies and Central America turned our lofty sentiments to pious hypocrisy, and the Latin-American nations jeered at our self-righteousness, and hated us for our power and ambition. But in each instance, the objectionable policy roused strong popular opposition in the United States. The policy of force was always initiated by the executive, and always, with the exception of the war with Mexico, in the end defeated by the Congress and the people. The popular belief in the freedom and dignity of the small nation always asserted itself, finally, to compel the administration to amend its conduct to greater conformity with the American people's belief in the co-ordinate position of all states.

Anyone who will examine the record will recognize that if the United States did not become a great territorial empire beyond its own shores, it was because the American people would not have it so. However, what is significant for our role in the world is not the refusal to follow in the footsteps of empire, trod through time by so many nations, but the grounds on which the opposition took its stand. For that is where our unique commitment to a philosophy of co-operation between co-ordinate states is, after the establishment of the Union itself, most clearly revealed. If we did not follow the alluring path of empire, it was because the American people recognized that they could only do so at the sacrifice of their own liberties, grounded in constitutional federalism, and in denial of their most cherished beliefs.

The first really serious attempt by a president of the United States to extend American control in the Caribbean followed the Civil War. General Ulysses S. Grant was bent upon annexing Santo Domingo. The justification in favor of such a policy seemed sufficient to the administration, but the proposal failed. This episode is illustrative of the grounds upon which this and the later expansionist projects were defeated. In favor of his plan, Grant argued the political convenience to the United States, the enhancement of American naval security to be derived from possession of Samaná Bay, the avoidance of the threat from European powers to the Caribbean island, and finally, the great natural wealth and resource that would accrue to the Union by annexation. The opposition was led by Charles Sumner of Massachusetts, then the most powerful member of the Senate. He rested his case upon an appeal to the governing tradition of the people of the United States—the co-ordinate character of the independent state. We had no moral right to deprive

71

another nation of its independent life. The words which he used are memorable because, in one form or another, they were to be repeated on every occasion when the question of intervention, or the threat of territorial expansion became an issue of public debate.

"Santo Domingo is the earliest of that independent group . . . towards which our duty is as plain as the Ten Commandments. Kindness, beneficence, assistance, aid, help, protection, all that is implied in *good neighborhood* [author's italics]—these we must give . . . their independence is as precious to them as is ours to us, and it is placed under the safeguard of natural laws which we can not violate with impunity."[1]

Sumner may have been warlike, aggressive, and oozing with hatred of Great Britain for its share in the arming of the South's cruisers, which had played such havoc with Northern commerce; he may have thought our acquisition of Canada would be an act of justice and pleasing to God himself, but then Canada was not an independent country. It was a colony, and no American since the War of Independence but considered colonialism an unmitigated evil. But when it came to Santo Domingo, that was something different. Santo Domingo was a free nation and therefore sacred, possessed of equal status, and must be treated as a good neighbor. This distinction between a colony and an independent nation is crucial in American thinking about foreign politics. A colony is something unholy, colonial power is bad power. It is opposed to freedom, independence, and equality. In good time, as John Quincy Adams thought, it would pass away.

This opposition towards colonialism is clearly seen in the case of Cuba. The hope that Cuba would, some day,

[1] *Works of Charles Sumner* (15 vols., Boston, Lee and Shepard, 1870–83), XIV, 124.

become a part of the United States was a continuing belief among American politicians and statesmen from the days of Jefferson to the days of McKinley. Successive secretaries of state and presidents, with few exceptions, can be cited in support of the argument that the United States had imperialistic ambitions against that Island. The consistent opposition to its transfer from Spain to any other European nation forms an important part of our diplomatic history. We were even apprehensive about the possible consequence of an independent Cuba, doubting its competence to maintain itself as a free state among the family of nations. But when the test came, during the Spanish-American War, when annexation would have been easy and seemingly logical in the developing course of events, President McKinley declared: "I speak not of annexation, for that cannot be thought of. That, by our code of morality, would be criminal aggression." And instead of fulfilling a century-old dream, rehearsed by nearly every administration, we accepted the Teller Amendment instead.

The Teller Amendment told the world, including the Cubans, that the American people were going to war to establish Cuba as a free and independent state. The Teller Amendment reads as follows:

"That the United States hereby disclaims any disposition or intention to exercise sovereignty, jurisdiction, or control over said island, except for the pacification thereof, and asserts its determination, when that is accomplished, to leave the government and control of the island to its people."[2]

The resolution declaring a state of war contained the sentence that the Cubans ". . . are and of right ought to

[2] Frederick H. Gillett, *George Frisbie Hoar* (New York, Houghton Mifflin Co., 1934), 200.

be free and independent." There was no suggestion in the debates in either the House of Representatives or in the Senate that the war against Spain was motivated by any desire for territorial expansion by the United States. This was true of the press. Even the most bellicose newspapers put their case on the grounds of humanity, on the necessity to bring the Spanish barbarities in Cuba to an end. The declaration of war was not taken by anyone, so far as the record shows, as a prelude to the conversion of the United States into a colonial power. In his instruction to Major General Brooke, President McKinley ordered him to govern, not in the interest or for the benefit of this country, but in the interest and for the benefit of the people of Cuba.[3] The Foraker Amendment (March 13, 1899) provided, "That no property, franchises, or commissions of any kind whatever shall be granted by the United States, or by any military or other authority whatever, in the island of Cuba during the occupation thereof by the United States."[4]

Our embarking upon a policy of imperialism was the result, not the purpose, of the Spanish-American War. It was during the war with Spain that the annexation of Hawaii was accomplished, and President McKinley wanted Hawaii annexed because of its importance to the defense of the Pacific interest so clearly dramatized by the war with Spain. But a treaty of annexation required a two-thirds vote in the Senate, and there was no assurance that such a vote could be had. To avoid risking a defeat it was decided, as in the previous instance of Texas, to accomplish annexation by a joint resolution in both houses of Congress.

[3] C. S. Olcott, *Life of William McKinley* (2 vols., Boston, Houghton Mifflin Co., 1916), II, 196.

[4] Bemis, *A Diplomatic History of the United States* (New York, Henry Holt and Company, 1942), 504.

The sources of opposition to the annexation of Hawaii stemmed from the same wellspring that in the end preserved the United States from becoming a great colonial power. Those who would keep us from following the paths of empire fall back upon the ideas expressed in the Constitutional Convention and upon the arguments rehearsed in the debate over the Northwest Ordinance. Senator George Frisbie Hoar, of Massachusetts, stated them for all those who would not forget them, even in the midst of the delirium of a successful war, that we are and can only be a nation of self-governing states. And Senator Hoar was a leading Republican, opposing the policy of a Republican administration. It was not, therefore, partisan politics that led him to say, ". . . if we are ourselves to be governed in part by peoples to whom the Declaration of Independence is a stranger; or worse still, if we are to govern subject vassal states, trampling as we do it, on our own great charter which recognizes alike the liberty and the dignity of individual manhood, then let us resist this thing in the beginning, and let us resist it to the death. . . ."[5]

Referring in this same speech to the Philippines, before the conclusion of the treaty with Spain, he said, "We will acquire no territory; we will annex no people; we will aspire to no empire or dominion, except when we can reasonably expect that the people we acquire will, in due time and on suitable conditions, be annexed to the United States as an equal part of a self-governing Republic."[6]

This, then, is the theoretical basis of opposition to American expansion during the hectic days of a strident and reckless mood that followed close upon the heels of the Spanish-American War and the coming to office of

[5] Gillett, *Hoar*, 206–207.
[6] *Ibid.*, 208.

Theodore Roosevelt by the unexpected death of President McKinley. Hoar's argument echoed the original theme in American foreign policy. It was to be repeated and elaborated in the dispute over the Philippines, over Nicaragua, Santo Domingo, and Haiti. It was the substance of what in the end proved to be the prevailing American policy: that we will not annex any people who cannot become an equal member of the self-governing Republic. The new territory will either acquire a co-ordinate position with the other states or it must be free.

The proponents of imperialism—and after the Spanish-American War they sprouted on almost every political stump—defended our adventure in colonialism on grounds of moral obligation and economic interest, but in the final reckoning it was Hoar's argument that prevailed. And it prevailed, not because of its greater logic, but because it reflected the belief of the people of the United States that a democratic federation can only survive "if the small states have an equal vote with the large"; that it can only survive if all of its members have a co-ordinate position; that it is not competent to govern other peoples against their will, and if it persisted in doing so, it would ultimately destroy itself.

As we have already seen, the Roosevelt corollary was criticized from its inception. It is worth examing how it was defeated. The new version of the Monroe Doctrine was stubbornly resisted in and out of Congress. The treaties negotiated and agreements entered into in accord with it were, in most cases, denied ratification by a Senate which opposed the attempt to foist an imperial policy upon a recalcitrant Congress and a strongly critical nation. This was true of Theodore Roosevelt, William Howard Taft, and Woodrow Wilson. The outbreak of the First World War, the long struggle over the League of Nations, and the election of 1920 overshadowed the new executive policies made to hinge upon the Monroe Doctrine. As soon, however, as the election of 1920 was out of the way, the Senate showed a growing concern over American intervention in Haiti, Santo Domingo, and Nicaragua.

The opposition in the Senate took various forms. The executive was attacked for pursuing an unconventional policy meant to serve the "Wall Street Bankers," that would impose arbitrary governments upon weak and helpless nations. The Senate appointed committees to hold hearings on the manner, method, and purposes of the interventions, and different senators made repeated efforts to attach riders to the naval bills, denying United States funds for the payment of the Marines stationed in the Caribbean countries.

The unhappy story of the American adventure in the Caribbean has been told many times and requires no repetition here. For our purposes, the gist of the matter is the ground upon which the opposition to the policy was made to rest. The basis of the reversal of the imperial policy merits careful scrutiny, for it touches the deepest beliefs of the American people. The explanations given by the several administrations to justify their intervention were never fully believed, were repeatedly challenged by the Senate and much of the public press on grounds that the policy was morally wrong. The people at large continued in opposition to colonialism, refused to be drawn into power politics, and denied that the relations between states can be helpfully maintained on any grounds other than those of good neighborhood. The hostility stirred in Latin America by "Yankee Imperialism" was a part of the basis of criticism. But the real motivation rested on grounds of conscience. It was an evil thing to impose a foreign government upon another people.

Active opposition against the executive policies began on January 15, 1922, when Senator Johnson from California asked for an investigation of the reasons for the intervention. He was soon joined by Senators King from Utah, and Walsh from Montana, and Norris from Nebraska. From then on senatorial criticism and obstruction continued until the Roosevelt corollary was formally repudiated in 1928 and the last Marines withdrawn in 1933.

During the intervening years, every new meeting of the Congress saw a renewal of the battle against United States intervention in the Caribbean. The running debate is a commentary upon American feeling and attitude in these matters. Senator Borah from Idaho, in condemning the manner in which we forced a treaty upon Haiti, and reading from a telegram from Admiral Caperton to the effect that the desired treaty with Haiti had been successfully negotiated ". . . by the exercising of military pressure at propitious moments," asked: "Can any man read that telegram and not feel a deep feeling of resentment that such a telegram should actually constitute a part of our history. . . . That telegram belongs nowhere outside of the archives of a military despot. I denounce it as un-American and indefensible." When Borah yielded the floor, Senator Ashurst from Arizona declared that "under the circumstances that treaty could very well stand side by side with Japan's treaty with Korea. . . ." Senator Norris remarked, "As a citizen of the United States of America, I feel ashamed of it."

The heated, and upon occasion, bitter dispute seemed interminable. Senator King expressed the feeling of many others when he said:

". . . Our military forces have no right to be in Nic-

aragua or in Haiti. . . . Nicaragua belongs to the Nicar-
aguans and Haiti to the Haitian people, and the inhabitants of those countries must work out their own economic
and political destinies."[7]

These debates in the Senate, repeated through the
years, are but part of the story. Each Congressional election brought additional criticism. The opposition newspapers, and even standard Republican sheets like *The
Springfield Republican,* criticized and condemned the
administration's activities in the Caribbean. To all of this
should be added the attacks on the policy in public meet-
ings, clubs, and the many memorials sent up to the Senate by groups of citizens who found the policy unsavory
and undemocratic.

Professor Dexter Perkins summarized this debate in
his restrained and careful manner when he said, "There
is, however, one interpretation of the Monroe Doctrine
that has never really met with the support of the American public opinion; I refer, of course, to the Roosevelt
Corollary."[8]

During the course of this debate, there were few indeed who gloried in our activities or defended them on
grounds of moral worth or political justice. Even the
ardent supporters of the policy argued only its expe-
diency, its necessity as the lesser of two evils, the other
being the presumed threat to the Monroe Doctrine by
some European power. No one suggested the permanent
occupancy of the Caribbean countries, and still less their
annexation by the United States.

The position of such upholders of the government's
intervention in Santo Domingo and Nicaragua as Sen-

[7] 70 Cong., 1 sess., 5428.
[8] Dexter Perkins, *"Hands Off"* (Boston, Little, Brown and Co.,
1941), 371.

ators Pomerene and Bingham is apologetic. Gone is the zest and forthrightness of such advocates of American expansion as Beveridge, Lodge, and Theodore Roosevelt. But more significantly, perhaps, the administration itself was in a penitent mood.

Speaking as secretary of state, in Minneapolis, on August 30, 1923, Charles Evans Hughes said that the United States had been trying to arrange for a withdrawal of its troops from Santo Domingo and Haiti, because "our interest does not lie in controlling foreign peoples; that would be a policy of mischief and disaster."[9]

President Hoover reinforced this statement by asserting, "We still have Marines on foreign soil. . . . In the larger sense we do not wish to be represented abroad in such manner."[10] The imperial adventure of the United States was drawing to a close.

Of greater significance, from the point of view of our inner commitment to the ideal of the co-ordinate state, was the course of events that so often brought the United States to the brink of war with Mexico. The controversy that began in 1910, under President William Howard Taft, lasted with only occasional abatement, up to 1942, when it was finally brought to an end by President Roosevelt. During these years, many American lives were lost in Mexico, and an investment calculated at one billion dollars was dissipated. Mexico challenged the right of the United States to extend diplomatic protection to its nationals, expropriated the oil industry, foreign holdings in agricultural lands, and, in effect, eliminated a large part of foreign participation in the Mexican economy, bringing serious loss for those Americans who, in the main, had in good faith invested their fortunes and some-

[9] Hughes, *The Pathway of Peace*, 137.
[10] *Foreign Relations of the United States*, 1929.

times their lives in Mexico. But in the end, the American people would not go to war with Mexico. They would not destroy an independent state in defense of "material interests"—to use a phrase of President Wilson.

When the crisis was at its height in 1927, the Senate declared by unanimous vote that the difference with Mexico should be settled by peaceful means. The senatorial vote came in the face of a recent declaration by President Calvin Coolidge that "the person and property of a citizen are a part of the general domain of the nation, even when abroad." What prevailed in the end was President Wilson's earlier declaration of United States policy towards Mexico:

"It is none of my business and none of your business how long they [the Mexicans] take in determining their form of government. It is none of my business and none of yours how they go about the business. The country is theirs, the government is theirs, and whilst I am President nobody shall interfere with them."

Theodore Roosevelt's boast, "I took the Canal," is less impressive than the fact that Panama was encouraged to set up as an equal member within the American family of nations. And after the Second World War, it exercised its equality by requiring the United States to surrender, much against its will, the use of air bases constructed for the defense of the canal. In some ways, the Panamanian rebellion is comparable to the secession of West Virginia during the Civil War. It is not a good instance of imperial conquest. And to appease our bad conscience, we paid twenty-five million dollars to Colombia.

The liquidation of the policy of intervention was begun under Coolidge and Hoover, and completed by Roosevelt. The Platt Amendment, supported and opposed with so much heat, was also repudiated. The American expansionist mood had evaporated in one generation.

The one real deviation in the application of the "fundamental principle" in this hemisphere is to be found in the annexation of Texas and the war with Mexico. Both of these events are so closely tied to the struggle for position between the slaveholding and free states that they do not make a clear case of repudiation of the "fundamental principle." The opposition to both was bitter. John Quincy Adams, "the architect of American foreign policy," signed a public manifesto opposing the annexation of Texas. Lincoln, Webster, and Clay, among many others, condemned the Mexican War and the acquisition of Mexican territory. Clay said: "This is no war of defense, but one of unnecessary and offensive aggression. It is Mexico that is defending her firesides, her castles, and her altars, not we." He then compared the war with Mexico to the partitioning of Poland.[11]

Abraham Lincoln introduced a resolution in the House of Representatives asking President Polk a number of pertinent questions aimed at establishing who was responsible for the war, and went on to add that if the President failed to answer, "I shall be fully convinced, of what I more than suspect already, that he is deeply conscious of being in the wrong; that he feels the blood of this war, like the blood of Abel, is crying to heaven against him. . . ."[12]

How bitter the feeling against the war with Mexico was may be illustrated by some extracts from a speech by Senator Thomas C. Corwin, delivered on February 11, 1847:

"You have overrun half of Mexico—you have exas-

[11] Speech of Henry Clay at the Lexington Mass Meeting, November 13, 1847 (New York, Printed by George F. Nesbitt, 1847), 14 pp.
[12] *Congressional Globe*, 30 Cong., 1 sess., Nov. 22, 1847, 64.

perated and irritated her people—you claim indemnity for all expenses incurred in doing this mischief, and boldly ask her to give up New Mexico and California. . . ."

"The Senator from Michigan [Lewis Cass] says he must have this. Why, my worthy Christian brother, on what principle of justice? 'I want room!'. . . . If I were a Mexican I would tell you, 'Have you not room in your own country to bury your dead men? If you come into mine we will greet you with bloody hands, and welcome you to hospitable graves.' "

"Why, says the chairman of this Committee on Foreign Relations, it is the most reasonable thing in the world! We ought to have the Bay of San Francisco. Why? Because it is the best harbor on the Pacific! It has been my fortune, Mr. President, to have practiced a good deal in criminal courts in the course of my life, but I never yet heard a thief, arraigned for stealing a horse, plead that it was the best horse that he could find in the country!"[13]

If one turns from the politics of the day and seeks for the objective judgment from the American historians upon the war with Mexico, he discovers that most of them condemn the spoliation of Mexico. They do not apologize for our aggression, explain it away, or justify it. They are writing about the acquisition of Texas, New Mexico, and California. But, instead of glorying in the addition to our territory, they ask us to hang our heads in shame. They are not Mexican historians, who in outraged patriotism are attacking the United States. No, they are American historians, some of the most distinguished among them, professors in the universities and teachers of the young. They are the keepers of our national con-

[13] *American History Told by Contemporaries,* ed. by Albert Bushnell Hart (5 vols., New York, The Macmillan Co., 1898), IV, 24–25.

science—a role that traditionally belongs to the historian —and they teach us that we have committed an unforgivable sin. Why? Because we outraged a weak, but independent and free nation. He who would understand the driving force that in the long run shapes our relation to the outside world needs to ponder this strange fact. Instead of being proud of a successful war and a huge addition to our territory, we are asked to be ashamed of it. Those responsible for the war, instead of being held up as heroes, are depicted as villains. Why? Because they willingly and deliberately plotted to commit an injustice. Because they attacked the weak and robbed the helpless. Because our historians, writing about American history, are themselves the unconscious exponents of the basic American belief in the dignity of man and in the equal right of the weak state to live side-by-side with the strong one. They do not believe in the current doctrine that might makes right, nor do they teach that security requires the powerful state to oppress the lowly one. The American historian has not fallen victim to the newer doctrines of power politics. That is why what they have said about the Mexican War is so important. It is a revealing insight into the character of the American people, and time has not changed the historians' critical attitude.

Hubert Howe Bancroft, speaking in 1885 of the Mexican War, says: "It was the result of a deliberately calculated scheme of robbery on the part of the superior power . . . to steal from a weaker neighbor a fine slice of lands suitable for slave labor."[14]

In 1887, David A. Wells thought our way against Mexico required "the vengeance of the Gods."[15]

[14] Hubert Howe Bancroft, *History of Mexico* (6 vols., San Francisco, The History Co., 1887), V, 307.

[15] David A. Wells, *A Study of Mexico* (New York, D. Appleton and Co., 1887), 261.

In 1901, Goldwin Smith described the war with Mexico as "the quarrel between the wolf and the lamb, and which no American historian of character mentions without pain."[16]

In 1904, James Schouler declared that ". . . under the smoke of defending the fourth part of Mexico we had just snatched from her to despoil her of another."[17]

In 1905, Cyrus Townsend Brady described the war as "the one serious blot upon our national history."[18]

In 1916, Henry William Elson declared that "no true American is proud of the Mexican War."[19]

Henry Steele Commager says that "Congress never declared war on Mexico. Polk did not dare to risk a vote on the matter. He had instead to simulate a Mexican attack."[20]

A number of other historians could be cited to the same effect. But the evidence is sufficient to indicate that the American historian has condemned the one clear deviation from our commitment to the ideal of the co-ordinate state. Some have recited the facts without either defending or condemning the Polk administration for its war on Mexico. But at least one troubled historian had to clear his conscience and find a justification for the war. He undertook the task of correcting the errors of the other writers on the subject because it is "the right of

[16] Goldwin Smith, *The United States: An Outline of Political History, 1492–1871* (New York, The Macmillan Co., 1901), 211–12.

[17] James Schouler, *History of the United States of America Under the Constitution* (7 vols., New York, Dodd, Mead and Co., 1904), IV, 526.

[18] Cyrus Townsend Brady, LL.D., *The Conquest of the Southwest: The Story of a Great Spoliation* (New York, D. Appleton and Co., 1905), 4.

[19] Henry William Elson, *History of the United States of America* (New York, The Macmillan Co., 1916), 529, 535.

[20] *Documents of American History*, ed. by Appleton-Century-Crofts (New York, 1949), 759 pp.

the American citizen to say to his boy: Your country never fought an unjust nor an inglorious war."[21]

It is clear that the story of the relations of the United States with its Latin-American neighbors have, in spite of many deviations, reflected the fundamental principle that lies at the root of its federal system. Whenever it has seriously departed from that commitment, opposition developed and in time forced a return to the traditional policy. In the one clear case of a violation of the belief of the American people in the co-ordinate position of the independent state, the war with Mexico, the American conscience has remained troubled, and the blame has been thrown on the slave power.

We find this view expressed by so distinguished a public servant and scholar as the late Henry L. Stimson. Speaking in New York before the Council on Foreign Relations in 1931, while secretary of state, he referred back to this period as an aberration "directly attributable to the influence of slavery in this country, then at the height of its political power."[22]

[21] Charles H. Owen, *The Justice of the Mexican War* (New York, G. P. Putnam's Sons, 1908) 8.

[22] Department of State, *Latin-American Series*, No. 4, 1931.

5

The Co-ordinate State
and the Far East

THE history of our relations with the Philippines illustrates once again the inner compulsions which shape our foreign policy. The annexation of the Islands was something of an accident and an afterthought. It was certainly not designed. In the debate on the Spanish Treaty ceding the Philippines to the United States, Senator Teller recalled that the Teller Amendment, adopted as we were going into the war and promising "to leave the government and control of the island to its people," only applied to Cuba, "but in principle it applied to every possession of ours acquired during this war. If any Senator had suggested that in addition to Cuba there should be added the words, 'or any other possession we may acquire during this war,' it would have met, as this joint resolution met, I believe, the unanimous support of this body and of the other, and also of the President of the United States, as is suggested to me by the Senator from Massachusetts [Mr. Hoar]. These words would have been added to the joint resolution with the approbation of all."[1]

President McKinley explained how sorely troubled he was when faced with making a decision about the

[1] 55 Cong., 3 sess., *Congressional Record*, XXXII, Part I, 325.

Philippines. We could not turn them back to Spain; we could not leave them a prey to other nations; we did not believe they were competent to govern themselves. The President confided to a delegation of the General Missionary Committee of the Methodist Episcopal Church: "I went down on my knees and prayed Almighty God for light and guidance more than one night. And one night it came to me . . . that there was nothing left for us to do but to take them all, and to educate the Filipinos, and uplift and civilize and Christianize them, and by God's grace to do the very best we could by them, as our fellowmen for whom Christ also died. And then I went to bed, and went to sleep, and slept very soundly."

But this pious explanation for an emerging imperialism suggested poor taste and a tinge of hypocrisy. It failed to satisfy and did something to scandalize the religious feelings of the American people. The Anti-Imperialist League, representing a formidable body of public opinion, including among its members Senators Hoar of Massachusetts, Carl Schurz of Illinois, and such influential citizens as Andrew Carnegie and Felix Adler, declared: "The United States have always protested against the doctrine of international law which permits the subjugation of the weak by the strong. . . . The United States can not act upon the ancient heresy that might makes right."[2]

While the President was explaining the inspiration that led him to disregard the "fundamental principle," one of his chief supporters in the Senate (Foraker) was saying, "I do not know of anybody, from the President to his humblest follower, who is proposing by force and

[2] Platform of Anti-Imperialist League, adopted at Chicago, October 18, 1899; from Henry Steele Commager, *Documents of American History* (New York, F. S. Crofts and Co., 1948), 192.

violence to take and hold these islands for all time to come."[3] Even Senator Lodge, who with Beveridge and Theodore Roosevelt was among the most vociferous expansionists in public office, declared that "the annexation will not commit the United States to hold an unwilling people for all time."[4] The bill for the annexation of the Philippines passed by a majority of one vote, and that slim victory was due, it is generally assumed, to the news of the rebellion of the Filipinos against the United States, which arrived the day before the vote was taken.

The Philippine Islands had been annexed. But in the debate that led up to the decision, there stands revealed, as clearly as anywhere, the American opposition to imperialism, the belief in the co-ordinate position of the state, the principle that we can take no territory except on the assumption that it will ultimately become of its own free will a part of the self-governing American federation, and the implicit promise that the Philippines, if they were to be annexed, would in time be given full self-government.

On December 12, 1898, Senator Vest of Missouri introduced a resolution which read as follows:

"Resolved by the Senate and House of Representatives of the United States of America in Congress assembled, That under the Constitution of the United States no power is given to the Federal Government to acquire territory to be held and governed permanently as colonies.

The colonial system of European nations can not be established under our present Constitution, but all territory acquired by the Government, except such small amount as may be necessary for coaling stations, correction of boundaries, and similar governmental purposes,

[3] 55 Cong., 3 sess., *Congressional Record*, 527.
[4] *Ibid.*, 559.

must be acquired and governed with the purpose of ultimately organizing such territory into States suitable for admission into the union."[5]

In the defense of his resolution, he ridiculed the "apostles of the New Evangel" of imperialism, who believed that we could hold other people ". . . as subjects, never to become citizens." The Declaration of Independence laid it down that "all governments derive their just powers from the consent of the governed." As long as we abide by that Declaration, it remains unacceptable for us to "govern millions, without their consent, as mere chattels" to be disposed of as the sovereign power of the mother country may choose.

In support of his argument that colonialism was not compatible with the Constitution of the United States, he cited that part of the Dred Scott decision which received the unanimous support of all the judges then sitting in the Supreme Court:

"There is certainly no power given by the Constitution to the Federal Government to establish or maintain colonies bordering on the United States or at a distance, to be ruled and governed at its own pleasure, nor to enlarge its territorial limits in any way except by the admission of new States. That power is plainly given; and if a new State is admitted it needs no further legislation by Congress, because the Constitution itself defines the relative rights and powers and duties of the State and the citizens of the State and the Federal Government. But no power is given to acquire a territory to be held and governed permanently in that character. . . ."[6]

This part of the Dred Scott decision, he recalled, had never been challenged or contradicted by any agency of

[5] *Ibid.*, 93.
[6] *Dred Scott* v. *Stanford*, 19 Howard 393 (1857), 446–50.

government or "one public man of eminence" until the last six months, when "the craze of expansion seems to have taken hold of the people of the United States." Senator Vest then went on to point out that the Northwest Ordinance, first introduced by Thomas Jefferson, made provision for self-government and for ultimate admission of the new territories as states into the Union. He also pointed out that similar provisions were contained in the Act of Cession in Louisiana, the Floridas, and of Alaska. "When, where and how have we ever surrendered the great doctrine that this is a Confederation of Sovereign States . . .?" Only four forms of government "are known" to the Constitution, the national, the state, the territorial, and the District of Columbia. He does not dispute the power of the federal government to "acquire and govern territory," but "I deny that territory can be acquired to be held as colonies. . . ." It is repugnant to the letter and spirit of the Constitution for the United States to govern millions of subjects who are not citizens, and to whom is denied all prospect of joining the Union as states. Colonialism is incompatible with American law, it is an appendage of monarchy, and destructive of free institutions. "It uproots . . . the basis of all republican institutions, that governments derive their just powers from the consent of the governed."

The opponents of colonialism had stated their case. We could acquire no territory which would not in time become an equal member of a self-governing federation. They repudiated annexation for constitutional as well as political reasons. The advocates of imperialism were hard put to it. Those who, like Beveridge, argued for it on the grounds of racial superiority, national destiny, and the American mission could be eloquent without being convincing.

The burden of the sponsors had to be carried by the legalist, by the skilled lawyer who could make out a case for the constitutionality of the annexation. That lot fell to Senator Platt of Connecticut. He argued that ". . . a nation has a sovereign, inherent, and unlimited right to acquire territory, because that is an essential element of nationality, and that to deny it is to deny our nationality. . . ."[7] And in reply to a question, he said, "I do not think there is any limitation upon our power to acquire territory." He insisted further that the right to self-government is a conceded and limited privilege which need not of necessity be considered as an inherent right. He was really very close to denying the original American proposition that government to be just must be derived from the consent of the governed. But that was a difficult position for a Connecticut Yankee to maintain.

When pressed by Senator Allen of Nebraska: "Is not self-government the inherent right of every American citizen, whether native-born or naturalized, or brought into our jurisdiction by some other means? Can we deprive him of self-government? Can we deprive him of the enjoyment of the same privileges and rights which we enjoy ourselves?" Then the cat came out of the bag. No, we couldn't. Here is the answer from the chief legalistic defender of American colonialism:

"I think that we may govern them . . . in the manner best adopted to their condition, and that will promote their welfare, and best educate them to the point where they will be capable of self-government." But this is, after all, only a doctrine of circumscribed tutelage which must lead up to self-government, to independence, or statehood. So that, even under the most doctrinaire ex-

[7] 55 Cong., 3 sess., *Congressional Record*, 287–88.

pansionism, we end up as we began, without a colonial empire. "I agree that in legislating for any of the territory acquired by the United States we are under moral obligations and constraint. We must legislate on the great principles which underlie our institutions, with liberty, justice, and the protection of individual rights in view. We must legislate in the spirit of republicanism, not in the monarchial or despotic spirit. We must legislate for the security of every personal right which the individual is fitted to appreciate and enjoy. In other words, we must provide for the people of any territory that we may acquire the most liberal, just, and beneficent government which they may be capable of enjoying, always with reference to their development and welfare and in the hope that they may be finally fitted for independent self-government."[8]

Senator Teller of Colorado was on the side of the annexationists. He was, however, troubled in his mind. The older American tradition would crop out. We ought to annex them. It was a kind of duty and glory. But ". . . we ought to keep in view all the time that some day these people are to be self-reliant and self-governing as we are, or that they may become a part and parcel of this Republic, entitled to all the rights, and subject to all the duties of citizenship of states."

This was the legislative as well as the moral background for the acquisition of the Philippine Islands. Our first serious adventure in overseas expansion was weighted with a bad conscience and with a broad commitment that the conquered people must someday become either completely independent or an equal participant in making laws for the self-governing federation called the

[8] *Ibid., Congressional Record*, 322 ff.

United States. And this commitment was immediately visible in the administrative and political history of the Philippine Islands.

In laying down the policy for the government of the Philippine Islands, President McKinley had said:

"The Philippines are ours, not to exploit, but . . . to train in the science of self-government."[9]

He followed this broad declaration by putting down in the instructions for the administration of the Islands:

"That in all cases the municipal officers who administer the local affairs of the people are to be selected by the people."[10] He ordered that wherever possible offices of wider jurisdiction should be filled by natives.

As early as 1903, William Howard Taft, governor general of the Philippines, declared, "The Philippines for the Filipinos," and a little later, after being attacked by American papers published in the Philippines because he favored increased use of Filipinos in public office, he said: ". . . Whether an autonomy of independence or quasi-independence shall ultimately follow in these islands ought to depend solely on the question, Is it best for the Philippine people and their welfare? . . ."[11]

We thus have, as early as 1904, the formal implementation by the American governor of the Philippines of the promise of independence, implicit in the great debate of 1898.

These ideas were reasserted by nearly every governor general sent to the Philippines. Francis Burton Harrison, appointed by President Woodrow Wilson, said that he was charged by the President to tell the Filipinos, "We regard ourselves as trustees, acting not for the ad-

[9] 64 Cong., 1 sess., *Congressional Record*, 603-10.
[10] *Ibid.*
[11] *Ibid.*

vantage of the United States, but for the benefit of the people of the Philippine Islands. . . . Every step we take will be with a view of ultimate independence." And the first step consisted in giving the Philippines a majority in houses of the local legislature.

These attitudes found their counterpart in an increasing participation by Filipinos in both local and general administration. Between 1913 and 1921, American officials were reduced in number from 2,623 to 614. The Jones Act of 1916 promised the full autonomy that was given the Filipinos in 1936. The debate on the Jones Act occurred while the First World War was raging, when it seemed to Americans that the bloody strife in Europe was illustrative of the evils of imperialism. The debate foreshadows the beliefs that ultimately took the people of the United States into the war, and suggests the reasons for their later refusal to enter into the League of Nations.

We cannot here follow this revealing rehearsal in detail. We must, however, cite a few excerpts from the speeches made in the United States Senate on that occasion because, as the reader will note, they reveal over and over again, and often in the simple language of a profound conviction, the age-old commitment of the people of the United States.

The debate in the Senate began on January 5, 1916.[12] Senator Shafroth of Colorado told his colleagues, in words that remind one of a speech by Lincoln, "We declared that all men are created equal, not in intellect, not in strength, not in color . . . but equal in rights. We said . . . that these . . . may not be invaded by others . . . cannot be bartered away even by ourselves. We further declared . . . that governments derive their just powers

[12] *Ibid.,* 502–869.

not from kings . . . presidents . . . parliaments . . . congress, but from the consent of the governed." He went on to add, "These fundamental truths will . . . persistently rise in our minds . . . to show our violation of the law of our own being."

Senator Thomas of Colorado echoed the persistent theme that "we must retain them as citizens, or we cannot retain them at all without doing violence to our form of government. . . ."

Senator Lippitt of Rhode Island pointed out that the platform of the Democratic party had, from 1900 on, declared for independence, as in fact it continued to do until 1936, whilst Senator Hitchcock of Nebraska insisted that there was no essential difference between the parties on this question.

There were, of course, other matters brought into the debate—the difficulty of defending the Islands, the expense of keeping them, and their small commercial importance. But these were not the most significant items in the discussion. If they had been, it would have been logical to give the Philippine Islands their immediate independence. But the Senate felt that the Islands were not ready for full political freedom. They were given greater internal political and administrative responsibility and were promised full autonomy, which was accomplished in 1936.

The American administration, because of its bad conscience and inability to assume that any other people are permanently debarred from either a competence for, or right to self-government and full national independence, saved the Filipinos their self-respect. The leaders of the rebellion against the United States became our chief supporters, and when the American flag was lowered and the Filipino flag raised, the people of the Islands spoke of *Ang Ulalin Watawat*—the orphan flag. When the crisis was upon us in 1941, instead of joining our enemies, they fought on our side. In spite of conquest, annexation, and foreign administration, the basic American belief in co-ordinate membership had made itself felt in the relationship that had grown out of the original conquest.

In some ways, this is the most eloquent testimony to our inability to treat any nation as a "subjugated" people. The episode came to an end with complete independence in 1946.

THE much older story of the "open door" in China, so characteristically descriptive of our way with the peoples of the world, led to the tragedy of a great war and to the contemporary heartburning of a "lost cause." What we have done in China, through more than a century, is so typically American that we probably could not have acted differently. We would not be a party to the destruction of a great nation. Our commitment to the ideals of equal status and the moral integrity of the nation led us to accept the challenge of a great and costly war. We really had no alternative.

This attitude towards China antedates the Open Door policy of Hay by nearly seventy years. In 1832, when Edward Livingston wrote out the instructions to Edmund Roberts, our first diplomatic agent to the Far East, he told him to inform the rulers of those strange countries that ". . . it is against the principles of our nation to build forts, or make expensive establishments in foreign countries," and ". . . that we never make conquests, or ask any nation to let us establish ourselves in their countries as the English, the French, and the Dutch have done in the East Indies. . . ."[13]

[13] Department of State, *Special Missions*, I, 73–75.

The agents of the American government have not always appreciated the commitments to nonaggression by the people of the United States and our belief that we must not impose by force upon other nations any doctrines or practices contrary to their own traditions. Our minister to China in 1854, Robert M. McLane, suggested that the United States combine with Great Britain and France in an aggressive policy to improve the treaty relations of the western powers with China and to secure greater commercial privileges. In reply, W. L. Macy, then secretary of state, spelled out for the benefit of the American minister what he should have known without asking. Mr. Macy said the President will have serious objection to the proposal because "the powers with which we should co-operate . . . not to call them allies, would have less reluctance to that mode of negotiation than this government." It would be of little use to send out a naval force in conjunction with other powers without authority to use if it intimidation failed, and if force were to be used, the authorization of Congress would be requested. But it was quite certain that a "case could not have been presented which would afford any hope that such authority could be obtained for it."[14]

Even more fully was the position of the United States towards China clarified by Secretary of State, Lewis Cass, to the newly appointed minister, William B. Reed. Great Britain and France were pressing China for a number of reforms that would improve the commercial and diplomatic position of the European nations. They wanted freer diplomatic access to the Emperor of China, an increase in the number of free ports, a reduction in the tariff, religious freedom to be extended to all foreigners, the suppression of piracy, and they wished these privileges

[14] Department of State, *Instructions to China*, I, 1056.

extended to all other "civilized powers." The American government was in sympathy with these objectives, and its co-operation had been sought by the British. Lewis Cass noted all of these facts in his instructions to Reed, and gave him copies of letters from Lord Napier, the British minister. Reed was instructed "to communicate privately with the British and French ministers upon all points of common interest, so that it will be clear that the three nations are equally influenced by a determination to obtain justice," and better protection for commerce with China. But Reed is told: "This country, you will constantly bear in mind, is not at war with the government of China, nor does it seek to enter that empire for any other purposes than those of lawful commerce, and for the protection of the lives and property of its citizens. . . . You will therefore not fail to let it be known to the Chinese authorities that we are no party to the . . . hostilities, and have no intention to interfere in their political concerns, or to gain a foothold in their country. We go there to engage in trade, but under suitable guarantees for its protection. . . . With the domestic institutions of China we have no political concern, and to attempt a forcible interference with them would not only be unjust in itself but might defeat the very object desired."[15]

The American concern for the territorial integrity and administrative independence of China was affirmed towards the end of that period in a way that has become an accepted formula in the conscious attitude of the people of the United States towards that country. It became increasingly clear towards the end of the nineteenth century that the great imperial powers were preparing to dismember China. Early in 1898, Charles Denby, Amer-

[15] 36 Cong., 1 sess., *Sen. Exec. Doc.* (Serial No. 1032), No. 30, 10–11.

99

ican minister to China, urged upon John Sherman (then secretary of state) that: "We should not hesitate . . . to announce our disapproval of acts of brazen wrong, and spoliation, towards China. . . ."[16]

Secretary Sherman did not act upon this advice. But with the coming of John Hay to the State Department, the older traditional formula of nonaggression towards China was given a more positive turn. And the advice of Charles Denby, urged upon the former Secretary of State, was, in fact, acted upon, even if not specifically adopted from that source. Hay's note of September 6, 1899, on the "open door" dealt only with commercial equality for all trading nations, and did not refer to the danger of Chinese dismemberment. In July, 1900, when the Boxer Rebellion increased the danger of Chinese dismemberment, the American Secretary of State made the American position clear beyond peradventure. He made every effort to limit the actual intervention to the suppression of the immediate uprising, the protection of the lives and property of foreigners, and the prevention of war with China. The foreign troops were withdrawn soon after quiet was restored.

It was in this connection that Hay used the now famous expression as representing our continuing policy toward China: "The policy of the Government of the United States is to seek a solution which may bring about permanent safety and peace to China, preserve Chinese territorial and administrative entity, protect all rights guaranteed to friendly powers by treaty and international law, and safeguard for the world the principle of equal and impartial trade with all parts of the Chinese Empire. . . ."[17]

[16] Department of State, *Dispatches From China*, CIII, No. 2858.
[17] *Foreign Relations of the United States*, 1901, Appendix, 12.

Referring to this policy many years later, Secretary of State Henry L. Stimson notes that: "These principles were not new in the foreign policy of America. They had been the principles upon which it rested for many years."[18]

Of the $333,000,000 indemnity against China as a result of the Boxer uprising, the United States claimed only $25,000,000, and in 1907, returned over $10,000,-000. The Chinese government set this part of the fund up to subsidize students wishing to study in the United States. During the Boxer Rebellion, the Russian government occupied Manchuria and refused to get out unless that territory was placed under Russian protection. Hay protested Russian occupation of Manchuria, as well as (February, 1902) her claim for exclusive mining and railroad privileges. He also objected to Russia's establishment of a commercial monopoly, her closing of Treaty Ports (April, 1903), and the exclusion of foreign consuls in Manchuria.[19]

The only deviation in a century-long policy towards China is to be found under the administration of Theodore Roosevelt, who made so many others in American foreign relations. In the Taft-Kotosura Agreement of July, 1905, Japan was given a free hand in Korea, and the Root-Takahira Agreement of November, 1908, "suggests," to use Professor Bemis's words, "that Roosevelt was preparing to give Japan a free hand in Manchuria as he had already done in Korea."[20]

It is worth noting that both of these were executive agreements and were not submitted to the Senate for confirmation. But Taft, who as President Roosevelt's per-

---

[18] Henry L. Stimson and McGeorge Bundy, *On Active Service in Peace and War* (New York, Harper and Bros., 1947), 249–50.
[19] Bemis, *Diplomatic History*, 488.   [20] *Ibid.*, 496.

sonal representative had agreed to hand Korea over to Japan, sought to safeguard China against further depredations when he became president. The means he suggested were perhaps not very promising, but the intent was clear enough. He suggested to Great Britain the desirability of providing a loan to China so that she could purchase the Manchuria Railroad, as ". . . perhaps the most effective way to preserve the undisturbed enjoyment of China of all political rights in Manchuria. . . ."[21] The loan was to cover the purchase of all railroads in those territories which were then under foreign lease or hypothecation as the means of preserving China's territorial integrity.[22]

Presumably, this same motivation led to Taft's approval in 1912 of American bankers' participation in the International Consortium then under consideration. United States participation would tend to protect China from the possible loss of her administrative unity and territorial integrity.[23] President Wilson, however, would have nothing of the International Consortium. Within two weeks after he took office, on March 18, 1913, he made the far-reaching public statement which reasserted the traditional position of the American people towards China. "The conditions of the loan seem to us to touch very nearly the administrative independence of China itself . . . and [are] obnoxious to the principles upon which the government of our people rest. . . ." He brought the issue back to the historical American position towards China. "Our interests are those of the Open Door—a door of friendship and mutual advantage. This is the only door we care to enter."[24]

[21] *Foreign Relations*, 1910, 234–35.
[22] Bemis, *Diplomatic History*, 497.
[23] *Foreign Relations*, 1909, 178.

Less effectively, but clearly enough, Bryan, in 1915, told the Japanese when they were pressing their Twenty-One Demands on China, that we ". . . could not regard with indifference the assumption of political, military, or economic domination over China by a foreign Power. . . ." This was written on March 13. On May 15, Bryan returned to the same question and said with greater force that ". . . the United States cannot recognize agreements or undertakings . . . between the Governments of Japan and China, impairing the treaty rights of the United States and its citizens in China, the political or territorial integrity of the Republic of China, or the . . . open door policy."[25]

In 1917, the Lansing-Ishii Agreement recognized that "territorial propinquity creates special relations," but both Japan and the United States declared that ". . . they have [not] any purpose to infringe in any way the independence or territorial integrity of China. . . ."[26]

The Nine-Power Treaty of 1921 brought the principles of the "open door" and the integrity of China, so long maintained by the United States, into a formal international agreement of the signatory powers, including Japan, Great Britain, and France. Those powers agreed: "To respect the sovereignty, the independence, and the territorial and administrative integrity of China; to provide the fullest and most unembarrassed opportunity to China to develop and maintain for herself an effective and stable government."

To Japan, however, the Nine-Power Treaty, the Pact of Paris, and the Kellogg-Briand Pact were in the

[24] *Treaties and Agreements With and Concerning China, 1894–1914,* ed. by John V. A. MacMurray (2 vols., New York, Oxford University Press, 1921), II, 1025.

[25] *Foreign Relations,* 1915, 105–11, 146.

[26] *Ibid.,* 1917, 264.

nature of plausible sentiments uttered to satisfy the mood of the moment. Japan was "realistic," it played the international game as the enthusiastic advocates of power politics think it should be played. It had a weather eye for its "national interest." It was not idealistic and was free from romantic nonsense. It had learned its lessons in the hard school of international diplomacy, and had taken its cue from the self-proclaimed followers of Machiavelli. When the right moment came, when the Western world was distraught by the economic hardships and political difficulties of the Great Depression, when the League of Nations was a council divided, when the United States and Great Britain had both permitted their navies to fall below even the permitted strength under the Washington Naval Treaties, Japan attacked Manchuria. It must have seemed a wise and courageous expansion of the "national interest."

China was weak, the United States was pacifist and isolationist, and Great Britain could not and would not fight alone against Japan in defense of China. The United States protested, Secretary Stimson reminded Japan of its signatures to the Nine-Power Treaty, the Kellogg-Briand Pact. That, however, had little influence upon the Japanese militarists. This was on September 22, 1931. A little later, on October 5, Stimson told the Council of the League of Nations: "On its part the American Government, acting independently through its diplomatic representatives will endeavor to reinforce what the League does. . . ." The League did very little that was effective. The period of the early thirties was not propitious for strong action by the League of Nations. Furthermore, the League of Nations was weak because it was not built on the principle of the equality of the co-ordinate state. The great powers used it to bolster their own system of the balance of power and for their seeming advantage. The Japanese pursued their fateful adventures and followed their "national interest" regardless of the judgment of the world.

The American Secretary of State, on January 7, 1933, sent identical notes to Japan and China. This was the now famous Stimson Doctrine. The notes said that the United States does not "intend to recognize any treaty or agreement . . . which may impair . . . the sovereignty, the independence, or the territorial and administrative integrity of the Republic of China . . . or the Open Door policy. . . ."[27]

The notes went on to say that we would not recognize any agreement "which may be brought about by means contrary to . . . the Pact of Paris of August 27, 1928, to which China, Japan as well as the United States are parties." America gave its adherence to the Lytton Commission's report which condemned Japanese actions in China. It also gave its "general endorsement" to the proposed settlement of the dispute. Finding that its aggressive behavior in China had been disapproved by the League, Japan "walked out." That, too, seemed "realistic" and in accord with the "national interest." The Japanese delegate to the League returned to Japan via the United States to explain to the American people the civilizing and pacifying purposes of Japan.

In 1940–41, the century-old story was drawing to a dramatic close. The American people had for fifty years at least—with only the temporary deviation under Theodore Roosevelt—maintained for itself and urged upon others the principles of nonaggression in China, of Chinese political and territorial equality and integrity. And now the great crisis was at hand, Japan offered not to go

[27] 72 Cong., 1 sess., *Sen. Doc. 55*, 53–54.

to war if we surrendered our commitment to the "open door" and territorial integrity of China. We had frozen Japanese assets and had placed an embargo against oil shipments. Japan had occupied most of China and had invaded French Indo-China. On November 20, 1941, the Japanese ambassador handed a note to Secretary of State Hull containing the conditions of peace for the Pacific. Japan promised to withdraw from French Indo-China in return for the lifting of the embargo, removal of the order freezing Japanese assets, and restoration of normal commercial relations. Those were the things Japan asked from the United States as a condition of peace. They seemed very simple and "realistic." Surely they would serve the "national interest" of Japan and would not injure that of the United States. But Secretary Hull and the American people thought otherwise. Their conception of realism and of the "national interest" rested upon an older theme.

The American Secretary of State replied as follows on November 26, 1941. "The Government of the United States and the Government of Japan, both being solicitous for the peace of the Pacific, affirm that their national policies are directed toward lasting and extensive peace throughout the Pacific area, that they have no territorial designs in that area, that they have no intention of threatening other countries or of using military force aggressively against any neighboring nation, and that ... they will actively support the following fundamental principles ... :

(1) The principle of inviolability of territorial integrity and sovereignty of each and all nations.
(2) The principle of noninterference in the internal affairs of other countries.

(3) The principle of equality, including equality of commercial opportunity and treatment.

(4) The principle of reliance upon international co-operation . . . and pacific settlement of controversies . . . , and that

The Government of Japan will withdraw all military, naval, air and police forces from China and from Indo-China."[28]

Japan's answer was Pearl Harbor, December 7. And so the story had come to its climax. The statement made by Hull in November, 1941, is not so different from the first one made by Livingston in January, 1832. ". . . It is against the principles of our nation to build forts . . . in foreign countries . . . we never make conquests. . . ."

Roosevelt and Hull fulfilled an original American commitment, not to be a party to the destruction of another nation. That was our policy towards China. It lacked realism according to the advocates of economic determinism and power politics. Well, Japan had its full measure of both, and it led straight to national suicide.

Why were we so idealistic as to insist upon Chinese national integrity at a moment when the "wave of the future" seemed to be so overwhelming? Our acceptance of the Japanese challenge involved us in mortal danger and the staggering military expenditure that no possible benefits from an Open Door policy would have justified. Nor is there any proof that, in the long run, our trade with China would not have been more prosperous under the political dominion of other nations than it actually was under the Open Door policy that we had pursued with such persistence.

The European nations and Japan were not committed

[28] Cited in Ruhl J. Bartlett, *The Record of American Diplomacy* (New York, A. A. Knopf, 1942), 633–35.

to the ideal of an Open Door policy, and their investment and trade were greater than that of the United States. In 1902 and in 1914, our investments were smaller than those of England, Japan, Russia, France, or Germany, and in 1931, they were only about equal to those of France and were exceeded by the other powers. American investments in 1914 were only $42,000,000 (not counting some ten million dollars committed by missionaries to religious and educational establishments). This represented only 2.8 per cent of our investments abroad. In the years between 1898 and 1914, when the United States defended Chinese integrity and kept the door open, its exports were (1914) less than 1 per cent of total exports, and only 2 per cent of total imports.

The imperial nations of Europe and Japan, whose vital economic interests in China were greater than ours, did not follow a policy of the "open door." Why not? The answer usually given is that the European nations at least were willing to fight for their trade privileges and to carve out special spheres of interest at the expense of China, and we were not. Why not? Because the American people would not support a war for the purpose of establishing a specially favored commercial position in China, or to establish a zone of influence, or carve out a territory and call it American when in fact it was Chinese. The American government could not use force for these ends, because the American people would not support that kind of a war. Why? Because the American people believed that the Chinese had a right to their own territory, their own government, their national dignity. And we would take only our share of equal opportunity for trade or anything else. To convert this position of ours into conclusive proof of economic motivation as the primary concern is a conclusion which could only be drawn in an age when economic determinism is the great obsession.

We differed from, and on various occasions objected to, the policy of imperial nations in China. We looked askance upon their special spheres of interest, their controlled ports, their claims to exclusive rights. We did not copy them. We staked out no claim and asked for no special privileges, not because we would not fight for them, but because the American people would not support what would to them have appeared an unjust war.

When, in the late thirties, Japan had closed most of the doors to China and left only the Burma Road, Great Britain agreed for a short time to close that, too. But we protested violently against the British compliance with the Japanese demands. It seemed to the Americans unfair and repugnant. Largely in response to our pressure, Great Britain reopened the road.

When the Japanese offered us peace in the Far East, at the expense of China, we refused. They even agreed to evacuate Indo-China if we would only recognize their conquests in China and Manchuria. We declined. Because of economic interests? No, because Roosevelt and Hull, speaking for the American people, recognized that no settlement which compromised Chinese political independence and territorial integrity would be acceptable to our sense of justice or consistent with our basic tradition. No American president could have satisfied the Japanese demands without risking repudiation, not merely by the opposition, but by his own party as well.

The American people accepted the Japanese challenge and the risk of war because they really had no alternative. The American people could not and would not become a party to the sacrifice of China. And that decision had nothing to do with the commercial advantages supposedly hidden in the Open Door policy. That decision, furthermore, had nothing to do with the defense of the "national interest," as defined by such contemporary students of international affairs as Professor Hans Morgenthau and George Kennan. It is not at all clear that our "national interest" was served by the complete destruction of Japan as a counterpoise to Russia, nor is it clear that, economically, it would not have been better—certainly much less expensive—to have permitted Japan to control and develop China. Our trade with both Japan and China would certainly have been greater, and we would not have fought a bitter war from which we have gained little but great military glory—something that Americans do not value enough to go to war about. To us, the "national interest" requires the survival of free and independent nations over the face of the earth. Roosevelt's and Hull's decision was inevitable because it was the decision of the American people. The old "fundamental principle" of the co-ordinate state ruled this decision as it has most others in our foreign policy from the beginning.

6

The Co-ordinate State
and the League of Nations

IN 1914, the United States had long been turned towards the paths of peace. The war with Mexico, the Civil War, the war with Spain had not led to the maintenance of large military forces. Our army was small and, in spite of its expansion after the war with Spain, our navy was moderate. Pacifism was widespread among the American people and highly respectable. The churches, the women's clubs, the labor unions, and many other organizations consistently preached pacifist doctrines and advocated the peaceful adjudication of difficulties among nations. Such leaders as William Howard Taft, Charles Evans Hughes, and Elihu Root stood committed to some sort of international league for the peaceful settlement of controversies between nations. We favored the World Court. Americans like Nicholas Murray Butler were conspicuous leaders of the international peace movement. Our isolation from Europe, our historical dislike of imperialism and colonialism were part of a moral disavowal of war and militarism.

The reaction of the American people to the outbreak of the First World War was incredulity. It did not seem possible that civilized countries like Germany, France, and Britain should undertake to destroy each other. Former President Eliot, of Harvard University, spoke of this "monstrous outbreak of primitive savagery." It seemed so futile. The almost instinctive withdrawal to neutrality was consistent with our tradition and, emotionally, an attempt to seal off any contact with the terrible tragedy. If the Germans had not violated the beliefs most sacred to the people of the United States, involvement in the European carnage would have seemed impossible.

One of the things that seemed incredible was the sudden invasion of Belgium and its complete and brutal subjugation by the German military. That act was seen by our people with absolute horror. Those of us who remember it still recall the complete incredulity that such things could be. Here was a peaceful little nation, bound by treaty to remain neutral, cultivating its fields, and following in quiet its own affairs, suddenly destroyed by a ruthless military, without a declaration of war, without cause, and in complete repudiation of a solemn treaty. The statement that the treaty was a mere "scrap of paper," uttered by the German Chancellor, confirmed the callousness of the German government. The burning of the library of Louvain, with its thousands of ancient books, aroused a feeling of abhorrence and symbolized the devil risen from Hell, to bring destruction to the earth. Americans never forgave Germany for that act of savagery, and the restoration of the library by the donations from the American people was a symbolic denial of the act itself.

The later course of the war and the institution of unrestrained submarine warfare was taken as a logical fulfillment of the original evil intent, as the Americans understood it. One must go back to the speech by President Wilson before Congress on April 22, 1917, when he asked for a declaration of war against Germany, to recall that we declared war, not against the German people, but against the apparition of an evil spirit in the world.

"The present German submarine warfare . . . is a warfare against mankind. It is a war against all nations. . . . we have no quarrel with the German people. We have no feeling towards them but one of sympathy and friendship . . . we are glad to fight . . . for the rights of nations great and small, and the privilege of men everywhere to choose their own way of life and of obedience. We desire no conquest, no dominion. We seek . . . no material compensation for the sacrifice we shall freely make."[1]

We went to war not to increase our power, not to expand our territory, not for aggrandizement, but to bring the evil spirit to heel, and make its reappearance impossible. It was America's war to end war in a literal sense. And it was that which took the people into it. How surprised the American people were to discover that there were secret treaties between European nations and that the allied powers were not, like ourselves, simply fighting to make war impossible.

SENATOR JOHNSON: Could you state whether or not any official investigation was made by our Government to ascertain whether or not there were any such treaties of territorial disposition?

THE PRESIDENT: There was no such investigation.

SENATOR JOHNSON: These specific treaties, then— the Treaty of London, on the basis of which Italy entered the war; the agreement with Rumania, in August 1916; the various agreements in respect to Asia Minor; and the agreements consummated in the winter of 1917 between France and Russia relative to the frontiers of Germany, particularly in relation to the Saar Valley and the left

[1] 65 Cong., 1 sess., *Sen. Doc. 5.*

bank of the Rhine—of none of these did we have (and when I say 'we' I mean you, Mr. President) any knowledge prior to the conference at Paris?

THE PRESIDENT: No, sir. I can confidently answer that question no, in regard to myself.

SENATOR JOHNSON: When our Government, through you, Mr. President, in January 1918 made the Fourteen Points as the basis for peace, were those points made with the knowledge of the existence of the secret agreements?

THE PRESIDENT: No. Oh, no.[2]

It may express our innocence, our naïveté, our childish lack of experience in the world, but to the American people the only thing that justified the war was the extirpation of German militarism, which was the great visible evil.

Wilson's Fourteen Points are part of the same story. They could only have been written by an American. The war could only have a moral purpose. It had to lead to a general association to guarantee the "political independence and territorial integrity" of great and small nations alike. Nothing else was worth the war. How clear this conviction was can be seen in Wilson's famous "peace without victory" speech, delivered before a joint session of Congress on January 22, 1917, three months before we entered the war.

This speech deserves the most careful consideration. The President of the United States was speaking for a nation at peace, striving to remain neutral, and giving utterance to the country's deepest convictions. He was, while arguing for peace, stating unconsciously the grounds upon which we would ultimately enter the war.

"It must be a peace without victory. . . . Only a peace between equals can last. . . .

[2] *The Nation*, Vol. CIX (August 30, 1919), 272ff.

. . . The equality of nations upon which peace must be founded if it is to last must be an equality of rights. . . . Equality of territory or of resources there of course cannot be. . . . But no one asks or expects anything more than an equality of rights. . . .

. . . No peace can last, or ought to last, which does not recognize and accept the principle that . . . no right anywhere exists to hand peoples about from sovereignty to sovereignty as if they were property. . . .

. . . I am proposing, as it were, that the nations should with one accord adopt the doctrine of President Monroe as the doctrine of the world; that . . . every people should be left free to determine its own polity, its own way of development, unhindered, unthreatened, unafraid, the little along with the great and powerful.

. . . These are American principles, American policies. We could stand for no others."[3]

For with us, security is only conceivable in a just world. That is where we differ from other peoples, and that is where the advocates of the doctrines of economic determinism and of power politics miss the point when they try to describe American motivation. To the American people, it is inconceivable that military security can rest upon injustice, upon power, upon the ill-gotten fruits of imperialism and oppression. Security must stem from the loyal co-operation of people associated in the common enterprise of peaceful existence in a recalcitrant universe. Power derived from conquest, exploitation, and abuse is insecure just because it is unjust, and is bound to fail when the crucial test arrives. The Fourteen Points of Wilson and the struggle in Paris for the making of the peace are illustrative of the issue at hand. The Fourteen

[3] 64 Cong., 2 sess., *Congressional Record*, Vol. LIV, Part 2, (January 22, 1917), 1741–43.

Points were the American expression of faith in a world where decent men could live together in peace and dignity and where the small and great states would feel secure.

The German government, after many misgivings and much heartburning, was finally driven to accept the Fourteen Points as a basis for an armistice. But after the Germans agreed, the Allied governments objected to them. The principles embodied in the Fourteen Points were not consistent with the existing secret treaties, and were not in the spirit of the traditional European diplomacy. Colonel House cabled to Wilson: "Clemenceau and Sonnino are not in sympathy with the idea of a league of nations."[4]

During the earlier discussions between the Allies on the armistice, the opposition to the Fourteen Points was very much in evidence. Lloyd George pointed out that the Germans had accepted the Fourteen Points "on condition of [their] being the terms of peace. . . . Should we not make it quite clear to the German Government that we are not going in on the Fourteen Points of peace?"[5]

Clemenceau, remarking that he had never been asked by Wilson whether he accepted the Fourteen Points, inquired of Lloyd George whether he had been, and was told in reply, "I was not asked either." It was suggested by the French Foreign Minister, Pichon, that they be set aside for the moment. Balfour indicated, however, that if the Allies agreed to a discussion of armistice terms without making it clear that they objected to the Fourteen Points, they would then be bound by them. Then said Clemenceau: "I want to hear the Fourteen Points,"

[4] Charles Seymour, *American Diplomacy During the World War* (Baltimore, Johns Hopkins Press, 1934), 369.
[5] *Ibid.*, 374.

and Sonnino, for Italy, added with some derision: "Yes, and the five more, and the others."

It required the threat of an American withdrawal from the negotiations and of possible direct communication between the United States and Germany, before the Allies would take the Fourteen Points seriously. "That would amount to a separate peace between the United States and the Central Powers?" Clemenceau asked. "It might," was Colonel House's reply.[6]

The issue remained serious enough for House to be prepared to warn them that if they did not yield to President Wilson, he would ". . . ask the advice of Congress whether the United States should make a separate peace with Germany, now that she had accepted the American terms, or whether we should go on fighting until Germany had accepted the terms of France, England and Italy, whatever they might be."[7]

The Fourteen Points were finally accepted with two reservations, and Germany surrendered.

The making of the peace, however, when the delegates gathered at Versailles nearly a year later, proved a different matter. Wilson's idealism and America's faith in a better world was there greatly compromised by the writing of terms which, in effect, largely repudiated both the purpose for which the United States had entered the war, and the Fourteen Points which Germany had accepted as a basis for ending it. When Wilson found himself faced with the realities of Europe, he compromised with the evil he had taken the American people into the war to destroy. He compromised in bitterness and in unhappiness. But he did it in the effort to rescue the League of Nations from the wreckage of America's hopes

[6] *Ibid.*, 376.
[7] *Ibid.*, 379. Quoted from *House Diary*, October 30, 1918.

and ideals. For, in the League, at least, there was the promise that in the end the ideals of the American people would be fulfilled. The League would make a world where the little nations could be as safe as the big, and have their moral integrity and political equality secured.

The American people, however, defeated this effort because Wilson had destroyed their faith when he yielded to European diplomacy. Had Wilson stayed at home, or had he abandoned the conference and declared in the ringing words he was master of, that he would not bargain with evil, that the American people had not gone to war to rescue the Imperial powers and guarantee them in their possessions, that he had not taken the people of the United States to war to destroy the German people but to save them and their conquerors as well from the dangers of future wars, he would not have lost his leadership, and he might have won both the League of Nations and an acceptable peace.

Colonel House emphasized this point. ". . . I do not believe that he utilized his commanding position. He was the *God on the mountain* [italics in the original] and his decisions regarding international matters were practically final. When he came to Europe and sat in with the Prime Ministers of the other states, he gradually lost his place as first citizen of the world."[8]

What in the end defeated Wilson, and the League of Nations as well, was not just political chicanery, or personal hatreds, or Wilson's stubbornness, but also the bitter disillusionment of the American people when they discovered that they had been misled, not by their enemies, but by their allies. The bitterness turned against France, but especially against England. And the League of Nations was ultimately voted down in the United

[8] Seymour, *American Diplomacy*, 399.

States Senate, not because it committed the United States to participate in world affairs, but because it sanctioned an unjust peace by tying up the League with the treaty. The League would seemingly confirm England, France, and Italy in their new gains. It would apparently increase the strangle hold of the Imperial powers over subject peoples. It would saddle French militarism on Europe. It would make a mockery of the proposed self-determination of nations, which was so large a part of the American war ideal, just as the treaty negotiations had made a mockery of open covenants openly arrived at.

It is erroneous to assume, as is almost always done, that the defeat of the League of Nations was evidence of our disavowal of interest in world peace or in world affairs. The League of Nations, tied in as it was with the German Peace Treaty, was defeated because it seemed to confirm the militarism we had gone to war to eradicate. One needs but to go back and read the debates in the Senate to realize that some of the most influential isolationists were objecting to Wilson's surrender of the cherished beliefs which had justified our going to war. One quotation will have to suffice.

We cite Senator Borah because he was one of the "bitter-enders." He was more consistent in his opposition than Senator Lodge, and refused to consider any compromise. He worked to defeat the League of Nations, not, as can be fairly said of some others, just to harm and discredit Woodrow Wilson.

Speaking on March 3, 1920, Borah said:

". . . Prior to the ending of the war . . . the President had announced the principles upon which world peace could be built. . . . They were the principles of a just settlement. . . . He went to Europe to engage face to face those whom he knew would oppose his policies and fight hand to hand against the ancient customs and prejudices of the Old World. He evidently believed he could Americanize European diplomacy, that he could give it a conscience and make it do service for democracy. . . . But in Europe he was compelled to accept Europe's views and in the end to adopt Europe's standards and systems. There is no use to deny it . . . this . . . is not the treaty which the President intended to give the world, neither is it the treaty which will bring peace to the world. . . .

Instead of a treaty based upon the humane principles of an American President it is a treaty preserving every vicious principle of European statecraft and through whose every page and paragraph, every open provision, and every covert phrase, vengeance crawls and writhes and hisses. A treaty which puts beneath brutal feet of power millions of subject peoples, and denies liberty and independence to countless millions yet unborn. This is the treaty which Europe exchanged for the treaty which America promised, and for which all the world waited."[9]

What defeated the League of Nations was, it is clear, more than President Wilson's stubbornness or his inability on his return from Europe to take the American people into his confidence. Nor was Senator Lodge's personal dislike of Wilson or the Republican party's effort to discredit the President the sole and sufficient cause for America's failure to enter an international association, long advocated by some of its most distinguished political figures, and brought into being by a president of the United States. For in the end, the League of Nations was opposed by those American liberals who had been its best friends.

The *New Republic* had supported Woodrow Wilson

[9] Senate, 66 Cong., 2 sess., *Congressional Record* (March 3, 1920), 3803 ff.

from the beginning, and was looked upon as something of a semiofficial organ of his administration. It was strongly in favor of a League of Nations. Before the great debate was over, however, it had joined Wilson's opponents and urged the defeat of both the League and the treaty which it embodied. This weekly was then in the heyday of its influence, and the opinions it expressed helped shape the thinking of newspaper editors and members of Congress. It is therefore of some importance to consider the grounds of the opposition of this journal.

In the early days of the debate, while still supporting the idea of a League of Nations, it said editorially, on November 30, 1918:

"If Europe is still to remain, as Senator Reed says, 'a maelstrom' of power politics, the American commonwealth would possess valid reasons for recovering her former moral neutrality and political isolation," and went on to argue that the essential point was that with a League, "Europe will no longer be torn by conflicting ambitions and irreconcilable animosities. . . ." If the League is to prove merely an alliance of the victorious powers for the suppression of the vanquished, then our experience with the war will have proven injurious to the United States, ". . . for we should have destroyed Prussia only to perpetuate Prussianism."[10]

By March 8, 1919, it was urging a revision of the draft of the League covenant, because it embodied the danger of our "renouncing freedom from the animosities" that so long warped the lives of the European peoples. The opponents of the League were justified, the *New Republic* argued, in so far as there was a danger that the American people might become entangled in a traditional system of European alliances.[11]

[10] *New Republic*, Vol. XVII, 116–18.
[11] *Ibid.*, Vol. XVII, 164–66.

"The danger is real. There are eminent statesmen in Europe and in America who are working ceaselessly to enclose them in the straitjacket of a traditional European alliance." By March 29, it had come to the conclusion that Article X, which according to President Wilson was the heart of the League covenant, should be eliminated, "because America should not be pledged to uphold injustice."[12]

The *New Republic*, therefore, long before the League was finally defeated, had taken substantially the same grounds of opposition that were voiced by Senator Borah.

The Nation, for so long an important influence among American liberals, supported President Wilson's domestic and foreign policies with enthusiasm. Like the *New Republic*, it was for a League of Nations and a just peace. It spoke of this being the President's hour, of his having been given a mandate by world events to establish a just peace. But as time dragged on, and the reports from Europe indicated that the ideals Wilson had propounded would not survive the peace conference, *The Nation* turned on President Wilson with increasing bitterness, and ended by being as hostile as his worst Republican opponents. The news that the League of Nations covenant was to be an integral part of the peace treaty was described as "a deliberate attempt to dragoon the Senate of the United States," and consistent with the "whole discreditable course of the Paris Conference."[13]

It went on to add that ". . . what we have is calm, arrogant, and ruthless formulation of a plan for world domination by the five conquering powers. . . . The governments of the United States, Great Britain, France, Italy, and Japan are the League of Nations; they are the

[12] *Ibid.*, 263–65.
[13] *The Nation*, Vol. CVIII, No. 2803 (March 12, 1919), 416–17.

executive council; they appoint the dummy directors; they pass finally on the qualifications of candidates; they are in short an absolute and irresponsible oligarchy."[14]

On March 19, *The Nation* said editorially, "The terms of the armistice were the terms of the secret treaties; the terms of the peace are the terms of the secret treaties."[15]

Without burdening the reader with further citations, it is clear that what defeated the League of Nations was something in addition to chicanery and the hypocrisy of much of the political opposition to Wilson. What finally assured America's refusal to enter the international association it had brought into being was the conviction that the League of Nations and the peace denied, rather than affirmed, the ideals of freedom, justice, and the independence of the co-ordinate state in the international community.

Wilson's effort to salvage something out of the wreckage led both to a moral and political disaster. The disillusionment of the "lost generation" that followed upon the heels of the futile crusade made America a lonely and isolated nation in more than the international sense.

We went into the war to "make the world safe for democracy"; we fought "a war against war"; we crossed the ocean a million strong to establish the principle of self-determination, and, when our allies confirmed what their worst enemies had said of them, we turned our backs upon them. We turned our backs upon them because they failed us. The League of Nations was but "a scrap of paper," and the real things were the secret treaties, the power positions, the economic arrangements, the

[14] *Ibid.*
[15] *Ibid.*, Vol. CIX, No. 2820 (July 19, 1919) 71 ff.

indemnities, and the cynicism of an older diplomacy that we could not understand and would not bargain with. We did not abandon Europe. Europe abandoned us.

There is visible in this prolonged debate the "fundamental principle" the American people have pursued with a consistency that is as surprising as it is fascinating. For this ideal of the co-ordinate state has worked in the things we did as well as in those we failed to do. In the struggle over the League of Nations, as we have just seen, opponents argued that Europe was irremediable, set in its corrupt ways, and incapable of learning the American lesson of equality and anticolonialism, and that we ought therefore to stay out of Europe. The advocate of the League countered that Europe had been reformed, Americanized, so to speak, and would now, if we joined the League, adopt our principles of the co-ordinate state, and then turn towards a beneficent rather than oppressive foreign policy. The "isolationists" and the "joiners" were arguing their case on the same grounds, the first insisting that Europe could not, and the second, that it could be reformed—reformed meaning learning to respect the political equality and territorial integrity of the independent nation.

7

The Co-ordinate State
and the Second World War

THE Second World War cast its black shadows before it and deepened the disillusionment of the American people with a Europe that could not abide in peace or tolerate the survival of freedom among men or independence among nations. The rise of Mussolini and Hitler confirmed the direst prognostications of the isolationists. The destruction of Ethiopia, the Hoare-Laval memorandum, the refusal to impose effective sanctions against Italy, the failure of the League to restrain Japan, the rearmament of Germany, the occupation of the Rhineland, and the annexation of Austria all testified to the seeming wisdom and foresight of the older opponents of "entangling alliances." President Roosevelt's quarantine speech in Chicago in 1937 fell on deaf ears; his warning that "the very foundations of civilization are seriously threatened" went unheeded, and the implied commitment in the statement that "those who cherish their freedom and recognize and respect the equal right of their neighbor to be free and live in peace must work together . . ." stirred the fear of a new involvement in a European world hopelessly bent upon self-destruction. But what hardened the American people in their determination to stay out of the European "mess" was the surrender by France and England at Munich. For here it was made evident that there were no moral principles left that were worth defending. The reaction in the United States was bitter, because the Munich Pact was a voluntary yielding of a principle of national integrity and political equality for which we had gone into the First World War.

American feeling reflected in newspaper editorials on September 20, 1938, when the news of France's and Britain's acquiescence in Hitler's demand for the Sudetenland was announced, suggested the course the United States would follow if a war should break out in Europe. The surrender to Hitler fortified isolationist feeling in the United States and was evidenced in newspapers scattered widely over the country.

The *New York Herald Tribune* said bitterly: "Humbly they not only laid Czechoslovakia upon the altar; they commanded her to commit suicide there. . . ."

The Washington *Evening Star* spoke in irate but prophetic language when it said: ". . . Paris henceforth speaks with the authority of Monaco. The Maginot Line has become a rope of sand."

To the Philadelphia *Inquirer*, the yielding to Hitler was a "sickening backdown," while *The Boston Herald*, like many other papers, recognized that: "The admonitions in Washington's Farewell Address will take on an aspect of gospel truth. . . . The hands of the isolationists will be strengthened." According to the *Richmond Times-Dispatch:* "The year 1938 will mark the beginning of the end of the British Empire. . . ."

The sense of defeat felt by Americans is reflected in the Chattanooga *Times*. The men who had died in the First World War had been betrayed by the Munich decision. This feeling was shared by millions of Americans. We had taken part in the First World War, and in testimony of our faith, thousands of our dead were moldering in European graves, only to have the things they died for surrendered by the nations we had crossed the ocean to save. "The Czechs are not alone among the betrayed. Millions of men who died in the World War in the belief that they were saving democracy have also been betrayed."

The Munich arrangement was barren of justice or merit, according to the *Times-Picayune* of New Orleans, and settled nothing. When Hitler precipitated the Second World War, France and England turned to the United States for help and sought in despair for the assurance that we would not let them perish. But the ghost of a sacrificed Czechoslovakia stood in their path and muffled their pleas. Most Americans saw not only the injustice of the Munich decision, but felt it to be morally degrading and politically unwise. But most of all they recognized, prophetically, the futility of the act. The Minneapolis *Star* remarked that "such a policy is bound to lead to greater disaster. . . ."

It is obvious that Americans talked and felt as if they had been betrayed and had lost a war. The revulsion in the United States against Britain and France, especially Britain, is only comparable to the feeling against Germany's invasion of Belgium in the First World War. It required the invasion of Denmark and Norway, the fall of France, and the heroic battle of Britain, now become a lonely little bastion against the forces of evil, to wipe away the guilt of the betrayal of Czechoslovakia. It would have been infinitely easier for the American people to have joined Great Britain in the war if she had, in 1938, thrown herself against Hitler on the grounds that she would not be a party to the destruction of an

independent little nation, that she would resist the growing evil to the bitter end. That would have been something we would have understood and approved, and in
the end supported. But to go to war in defense of allies
guilty of betraying the moral principles which, to the
American people, alone justify a great national sacrifice
proved a different thing indeed. The threat implicit in
a German victory had to become stark clear before the
American people could be moved to support Great
Britain.

In 1939, when Roosevelt, who clearly saw the meaning of the Nazi threat, addressed himself to Hitler and
Mussolini to secure from them the terms of a possible
peace, he used language that spelled out the old American tradition in favor of the security of the independent
nation. "Three nations in Europe and one in Africa have
seen their independent existence terminated. . . . Are you
willing to give assurance that your armed forces will not
attack or invade the territory or possessions of the following independent nations: Finland, Estonia, Latvia,
Lithuania, Sweden, Norway, Denmark, the Netherlands,
Belgium, Great Britain and Ireland, France, Portugal,
Spain, Switzerland, Lichtenstein, Luxemburg, Poland,
Hungary, Rumania, Yugoslavia, Russia, Bulgaria, Tur-
key, Greece, Iraq, the Arabias, Syria, Palestine, Egypt,
and Iran." We repeat the list because it reasserts in specific terms the implicit idea of the co-ordinate state. For
it was on this basis that we were ultimately to go to war.

This doctrine was stated once again in 1940, this
time against Russia when she occupied the Baltic countries. Sumner Welles told the Russians, "The people of
the United States are opposed to predatory activities . . .
to any form of intervention on the part of one state, however powerful, in the domestic concerns of any other

state, however weak. These principles constitute the very foundation upon which the existing relationship between the twenty-one sovereign republics of the new world rests. The United States will continue to stand by these principles *because of the conviction of the American people that unless the doctrine in which these principles are inherent once again govern the relations between nations . . . modern civilization can not be preserved.*[1] [author's italics]

The theme of the co-ordinate state is thus projected for the rest of the world. It is the older ideal of Wilson to extend the Monroe Doctrine through a league to all nations. It is the same doctrine which, in 1941, appears in the Atlantic Charter. And the commitments in the Atlantic Charter—statements of the proposition of equality, freedom, and independence of the little state along with the great—are what gave the Second World War something of the same crusading flavor that the First World War had.

These restatements of American ideals had little immediate influence upon the course of the Second World War. While President Roosevelt was asserting in simple and moving words the devotion of the people of the United States to the Christian philosophy of human dignity and justice among men and nations, the darkness was closing in on the world. Hitler's armies had destroyed Poland, overrun France, conquered Belgium and Holland, occupied Norway and Denmark, subjugated Yugoslavia and Greece, and crossed the Mediterranean to threaten Egypt and the Suez Canal. In the Far East, Japan had placed nearly all of China beneath the yoke, and extended its hold upon most of Indo-China, and was

[1] *Documents on American Foreign Relations* (Boston, World Peace Foundation, 1940), III, 429-30.

threatening the Malay Peninsula. There seemed nothing in the way to stop them from overwhelming Australia and New Zealand. The entire world was threatened by Germany and Japan. Only two major powers, Russia and the United States, were not engulfed by war, and Russia had signed a treaty of friendship with Germany and had taken her share of partitioned Poland once again.

Britain alone fought on against the day of certain doom, unless the American people came to her aid. The American people watched the Battle of Britain with increasing admiration and growing apprehension. They were, in their vast majority, opposed to totalitarianism and contemplated the prospect of a German and Japanese victory with increasing distrust. But a large part of the American people were isolationist. Their experience in the First World War had heightened their skepticism of the integrity of European statesmen and increased their dislike of power politics. They had fought one war in Europe for the ideals American people take for granted, and the fruits of the victory were denied them. And here, once again, while the wounded from the last war were still filling thousands of hospital beds, the call was on them to cross the ocean once more to do battle against the evil powers they had once reduced. They were asked, as they had been before, to go forth and lay down their lives to "save the world for democracy!" Yes, but what about Munich, what about Czechoslovakia, Ethiopia, Ireland, India, and the other peoples of Asia and Africa held in bondage by the nations we were now to save once again? With the greatest of difficulty, President Roosevelt had succeeded in getting Congress to repeal the Arms Embargo Act so as to permit Great Britain to purchase arms and food in the United States. But that was obviously insufficient; if Great Britain was to hold on at the edge of the precipice, we would have to become the "Arsenal for Democracy."

The conclusive debate in Congress on what we should do to halt the growing totalitarian menace came over the Lend-Lease bill in February, 1941. It proved to be a rehearsal of the earlier arguments over the League of Nations. There seemed to be nothing to add to what had previously been said. Those who favored President Roosevelt's desire to help Great Britain to survive and to defeat the unholy ambitions of Germany, repeated the American commitment to defend democracy and maintain the independent state. They said, over and over again, that the survival of democracy and respect of national integrity in the rest of the world had always been a matter of deepest concern to the United States. In fact, if we were ever to have peace, democracy and the respect for little nations must not be allowed to disappear from the face of the earth. A totalitarian victory would endanger the existence of the United States just because we could have no friends and no allies except among the democracies, whom we must preserve, to perpetuate the only kind of a world that we could live in with any prospect of peace.

The opponents of the measure, the isolationists, argued as had been argued previously, that Europe was doomed to constant war, that it never had and never would respect the independence of weak nations, that each was driven by the same hateful ambition to control and dominate other nations, and England, whom we would now defend, had just as bad, if not a worse, record of imperialism as her enemies. It was no use to take American lives and expend them in Europe to defend democracy, freedom, and independence. Europe was, and would remain, incorrigible. So, once again, those who favored and those who opposed a major change in American foreign policy were doing it on the same grounds.

The debate speaks for itself. We cannot follow it because it adds nothing new to the argument. Two citations will illustrate the theme of this book—that we always repeat the same body of ideas every time we are called upon to deal with international questions.[2]

Senator Thomas of Utah argued that the proposal was consistent with our traditional foreign policy, which derives from the Declaration of Independence.

"The fundamental principle of International law— and without that principle there can be no international law—is that, regardless of the size of the state, regardless of its power, the state shall be recognized as an entity on an equal basis with every other state."

La Follette of Wisconsin insisted about England: "... When it was to her interest in Asia to allow Japan to take Manchuria, she did so. When it was to her interest in Africa to allow Mussolini to take Ethiopia, she did so. When it was to her interest in Europe to allow Hitler to take Austria and Czechoslovakia, she did so."

It is clear that those who urged aid to England did so because they were anxious to defeat tyranny, to maintain the principle of freedom, and the right of little nations to live in independence. They also believed that in saving the democratic nations they were serving the best interests of the United States.

It is equally clear that many of those who opposed Lend-Lease did so because they hated imperialism and tyranny, and could see no grounds for holding English rule in India, or the history of English relations with Ire-

[2] 77 Cong., 1 sess., *Congressional Record*, Vol. LXXXII, Part I (February 17 and 19, 1941), 1033–58, and 1151–71 *(House Report 1776)*.

land or Egypt as evidence of Britain's commitment to freedom and independence. They called up the surrender of independent territories to Japan, Italy, and Germany as a proof of English indifference to the ideal of freedom. They recalled the refusal to write a peace on Wilson's Fourteen Points as a betrayal that would be repeated again if we got involved in the Second World War, and they argued that Europe was irremedial, and that America could not change European political habits, and would only risk its own security and democracy by becoming entangled in European wars.

All of this was said by men who repeatedly avowed their hatred of tyranny, war, and oppression. Their evaluation of the political forces at play in the world may be questioned, but what remains clear is that those who argued in favor, and those who opposed Lend-Lease, were basing themselves on the same principles—the ideal of freedom and equality among co-ordinate states.

Pearl Harbor brought a temporary end to the debate between the isolationists and the interventionists. The differences that had so deeply divided the American people were merged in a common effort to defeat the totalitarian forces that threatened to conquer the earth.

In stating America's purpose in the war, President Roosevelt and his associates repeated what had been said a hundred times before. The war must not only be fought to the utter defeat of the enemy, but out of it must emerge a world of freedom and justice, where the little nation can live in peace and dignity beside its large neighbors. Fear of aggression must pass from the world, and an international body competent to maintain the peace must be brought into being to assure that justice and freedom shall prevail among nations.

These ideals are then repeated in the Moscow Declaration and in statements issued after the Teheran Conference. They are also embodied in the basic principle of the United Nations: "The Organization is based upon the principle of the sovereign equality of all its members."

President Truman repeated these same principles in outlining the fundamentals of American foreign policy in his speech of October 27, 1947, when he said: "We shall refuse to recognize any government imposed upon any nation by the force of any foreign power"; and in the Truman Doctrine, when he declared that "one of the primary objectives of the foreign policy of the United States is the creation of conditions in which we and other nations will be able to work out a way of life free from coercion." These same doctrines are implicit in the North Atlantic Treaty, in the mutual defense assistance policy, and in President Eisenhower's proposal to condemn Russia's violation of the Yalta and Potsdam agreements. The "fundamental principle" of co-ordinate states, with which our history as a federal union began, has thus remained a continuing philosophy of international relations up to the present.

Characteristically American has been the popular reaction to the deviations in our basic attitude which have followed some of the decisions made at the Yalta Conference. The announcement by the White House that the United States had agreed to the Russian demand for three votes in the General Assembly of the United Nations and had accepted an equal number of votes for itself was announced on March 29, 1945, and repudiated on April 3—a major policy reversal in five days. This change of a basic political decision reflects the strength of the opposition to a proposal which would have violated the principle of equality upon which our nation rests, and upon which the Pan-American system has been built. The acceptance of the great-power veto has been subjected to constant criticism from the beginning. It had to be officially defended by Secretary of State Stettinius, and has, in effect, on the initiative of the United States, lost much of its controlling weight by the transfer to the Assembly of vital questions upon which decisions could have been blocked by the exercise of the veto by Soviet Russia. The fact that the transfer of jurisdiction from the Security Council to the Assembly was in the effort to protect the sovereignty and integrity of an independent nation—Korea—is eloquent testimony to the soundness of the historical American tradition of the co-ordinate state.

The criticism which applies to the veto applies to the rule of permanent membership of the great powers in the Security Council. It seems to many Americans just as unreasonable as it would have been for the Constitutional Convention to have named the states of New York, Pennsylvania, Massachusetts, and Virginia as the great states with special powers and responsibilities, a proposition made during the debates and rejected. In San Francisco, the Latin-American nations, when they objected to the veto, the great power designation, and to multiple votes for Russia, were in effect repeating the role in the discussion of the constitution of the United Nations that the little states played in the formation of the federal Union. It is predictable that if the United Nations is to survive, it will in time adopt, perhaps in stages, the proposition of co-ordinate membership in its fullest sense. For one thing is clear: the American federal Union and the Pan-American system have grown stronger with the years because the principle of equality removed the one fundamental obstacle to international co-operation—an equal opportunity to participate in a decision which affects all the member nations.

The principle of the "indestructible" state is the fundamental condition for the "indestructible" union. The American people have followed this ideal from the beginning and can, in fact, follow no other. That is what the world means to them. The bitter attack upon the Yalta agreement to give Russia certain special rights in China is a good example of the American position. The criticism, in spite of the justifying reasons of the military demands of a great war, is on the grounds that it was done without China's knowledge and consent. No crisis, in the minds of Americans, justified our giving away parts of another peoples' territory without its own previous agreement. For Americans believe that the principle of equality, by providing an equal opportunity to participate in a decision which affects all members, removes the most important obstacle to international co-operation. There is neither an alternative nor a substitute for the strength that comes with union. But a true union depends upon voluntary adhesion, only possible among those possessed of equal dignity.

It would be good for the world, and for ourselves, to be clear about the concrete significance of this tradition at the present moment. Americans want peace with Russia, but will not buy it at the expense of other nations. The American tradition has no room for a settlement which would divide the world into spheres of influence. It has no room for the sacrifice to Russia of any nation, small or large, for the sake of securing an abatement of the "cold" war, or for the sake of avoiding a hot one. The only kind of peace acceptable to it is based on collective security—again, the principle of the co-ordinate membership of all states in the family of nations. Much misunderstanding would be avoided if, in their reasoning about us, our friends began with that simple fact.

The enormous energy of the United States has been disciplined by the ethical conception of political equality, and harnessed to the ideal of collective security resting upon a federation of co-ordinate states. These are the grounds of our difference with Russia. We are not quarreling over economic interests, political doctrines, or her internal policies, even if we do not like them. We cannot accept Russia's denial of the co-ordinate character of other states. We do not believe in the Big Five, the Big Three, or the Big Two. The day the Soviet Union learns, if it can, to accept its neighbors as of equal rank with itself, the world will be united again, and the Iron Curtain will melt into thin air. Our quarrel is not about Russia, but about her contempt for the independent sovereignty of other nations.

☆ 8 ☆

The Doctrine of the
Co-ordinate State

THE philosophy of foreign relations presented in previous chapters is meant to illustrate the impact of a particular body of experience, and not to praise American idealism. An international society, built upon the co-ordinate state, must of necessity behave differently from one resting upon the concept of centralized power. The first makes co-operation both the means and the end of its policy. It can, in fact, have no other objectives. Its ends are determined by its means. Its objectives in international, as in internal affairs, can only be co-operation for the resolution of common difficulties, and its means can again only be co-operation. It accepts the doctrine of live and let live as a matter of course, for its own life is conceived of as a process of continuing accommodation within a world of nonviolent friction.

Friction and differences are taken for granted. They are recognized as a persistent phenomenon. There is no effort at an absolute or perfect solution. The very meaning of peace is unwittingly redefined to mean, not the absence of serious difficulties, or the disappearance of differences of interest, but the daily haggling over issues towards a workable compromise. An international society composed of "equal" members endowed with unequal resources requires the surrender of the "simplistic" notion of a "solution" of "problems." The very notion of "solution" and the concept of "problem" for which a permanent "solution" is to be had are both felt to be delusive. There are no "problems" and no "solutions" in the complex of political society or in international relations. There are, in fact, no "social sciences" from which these final ends can be derived. And the beginning of wisdom in these matters is the recognition that man abides in a recalcitrant and imperfect universe.

The world is not fully malleable to the hand of man. All of life, all of society, all of international relations is a developing and changing series of forces upon which no stable form can be imposed by any method. The best that man may contrive are means towards a workable compromise so that change may occur without violence. Friction will go on, differences old and new will continually emerge, and no formula the "scientists," politicians, and statesmen can devise will freeze the fleeting moment and permanently balk the hidden and contradictory flux that always moves through the world, and must do so as long as man survives on the face of the earth. These contradictory processes are life itself. If they ceased to be, life—personal, social, or international —would also cease. The feasible is not a permanent "solution," but a channel for continuing adjustments among contradictory drives.

A substantial amount of balance between the forces of nature is essential to survival, but the balance is never absolute and is always changing. A stable world is best described as one of relative instability. It is in that sense that there are no solutions and no problems, either within the nation or between the nations. But these compromises can only be made between recognized and existing entities. These entities must not only exist, but be recognized as existing, whether they be men, institutions, societies, corporations, or nations. The recognition of their existence implies an acknowledgment of a claim upon all other similar beings because they can only survive mutually, and cannot live in absolute isolation. The condition of mutuality is an equal opportunity to survival, which in turn requires the acceptance of the equal dignity of the existing entities mutually interdependent.

This is the meaning of the "co-ordinate state" in international relations. It implies a position of equal dignity. It has nothing to do with wealth, power, size, population, or culture. It has everything to do with the recognition that compromise is a continuing means of nonviolent friction (peace). It has everything to do with the acknowledgment of the unique sense of "historic personality" which each state has of itself as the only basis of a friendly relationship. It is only if all the states continue to have equal dignity among themselves that changes in power and wealth can be absorbed without undue violence. That is the essence of federalism in international relations. The co-ordinate state relationship makes it possible to accept the inevitable growth of some and the decline of other states without war and without the loss of "face," because the changes are gradual and absorbed through a process of accommodation by all the members who are equal to each other. Federalism embodies these traits and has been illustrated in many ways by the history of the United States.

The essential character of the American system derives from a federal relationship of co-ordinate states. Our expectations and demands upon the world are conditioned by that fact. This does not mean that we have not, in our relations to the outside world, committed grave errors and on many occasions denied our own beliefs. The traditional twisting of the "British Lion's tail" is but one example of a species of irresponsibility in international relations: Theodore Roosevelt's interference in the arbitration of the Alaska boundary dispute; his "I took the Panama Canal"; Wilson's intervention in Haiti and Santo Domingo; the Platt Amendment; the arbitrary senatorial action on Japanese migration; the almost century-long bullying of Mexico; the numerous landings of American Marines in Central America; the indifference to the feelings of foreign nations often expressed in Congressional debates; our constant preachments and moralizations; the subordination of our foreign policies to domestic politics; the support of "big business" and American investors in foreign countries, sometimes without due regard to the legitimacy of their claims; the lack of sensitivity to foreign culture and foreign values, and since the Second World War, the conscious but faltering support of colonialism, are all part of the story of our failure to abide by our own commitments.

However, these variations from our own professed ideals are the side currents at the edge of the broad stream of our foreign policy. The major drift of our relations with the rest of the world have, with more or less consistency, responded to the basic tradition of the co-ordinate state. We have, with the exception of the short but more memorable episode of the Freedmen's Bureau and Reconstruction, never for long deviated from the idea of equal dignity of the state inside our own federal system, and have, therefore, never long permitted ourselves to act overtly towards other nations as if we were a centralized state, concerned primarily with the security that rests upon military force and military alliances. We have always sought our security either in isolation or in cooperation with other nations of equal dignity.

This conception of the equal dignity of the state is therefore fundamental to our own thinking about the world. Just what do we mean by the equal dignity of the state? This is a crucial question, for it defines the character of our own federal system. More than that, this concept of the equal dignity of the co-operating state represents a basis, not merely for our own federal system, but lies at the root of the Organization of American States. What is more, it is a similiar concept, not uninfluenced by the American experience which has come to govern the Commonwealth of Nations. This same basic definition of the equal dignity of the related members has shaped the long-successful Swiss Federation. We are, therefore, dealing with a general principle of organization, of which the American federal system is but a type. And this system of international organization stands in the world as a contrast to the alternative idea of the balance of power between states, and to the doctrines of power politics advanced by the schools of *realpolitik,* of which Professor Hans J. Morgenthau and Mr. George F. Kennan are, at the moment, the most widely recognized proponents in the United States.

The nature of the American system of relations between states of equal dignity was, as we saw in the second chapter, first discussed in the Continental Congress and in the Constitutional Convention. It was even more significantly reaffirmed in the great controversy known in our history as the Missouri Compromise. The question at issue was whether the Congress of the United States could lay a permanent limitation upon a new state which infringed upon its sovereignty to the extent of making it a state of lesser power and dignity than the original states which had formed the Union. The immediate issue was that of slavery; the larger question was that of the constitutional powers of the Congress to create within the federal Union states of lesser legal prerogative, and, therefore, inferior in rights and dignity to the other members of the same Union. It was on this proposition that the matter was fought out, and the upholders of the equal sovereignty of the states in the federal Union won the battle, with the support of those representatives and senators from the North who recognized the constitutional implications of the debate. For what was being argued was whether the federal Union, framed within the Constitution, should now be transferred into a different government, where, by an act of Congress, varying categories of states could be made to arise within the federal system.

On that issue a number of the antislavery members of Congress voted with the proslavery members in favor of the proposition that Congress could only admit states possessed of equal status with those already in the Union. Otherwise, Congress would acquire the power to "make mere provinces" of the new commonwealths.[1]

It was successfully argued that the Congress could not change the character of the federation by "selling the territories a license to the commonweal status,"[2] and in return acquire powers over the new states that it did not possess over the older members of the Union.

The case for the co-ordinate position of each of the states was stated with great force and eloquence by Senator William Pinkney of Maryland:

"What is this Union? A confederation of States, equal in sovereignty, capable of everything which the Constitution does not forbid, or authorize Congress to forbid.

[1] John W. Burgess, *The Middle Period, 1817–1858* (New York, Charles Scribner's Sons, 1910) *The American History Series*, 70.
[2] *Ibid.*, 80

It is an equal union between parties equally sovereign. They were sovereign, independent of the Union. The object of the Union was common protection for the exercise of already existing sovereignty. The parties gave up a portion of that sovereignty to insure the remainder. As far as they gave it up by the common compact, they have ceased to be sovereign. The Union provides that means for securing the residue; and it is into *that* Union that a new State is to come. By acceding to it, the new State is placed on the same footing with the original States. It accedes for the same purpose, that is, protection for its unsurrendered sovereignty. If it comes in shorn of its beams, crippled and disparaged beyond the original States, it is not into the original Union that it comes, for it is a different sort of Union. The first was a Union *inter pares*. This is a Union *inter-disparates*, between giants and a dwarf, between power and feebleness, between full proportioned sovereignties and a miserable image of power—a thing which that very Union has shrunk and shrivelled from its just size instead of preserving it in its true dimensions. It is into *this* Union, that is the Union of the Federal Constitution, that you are to admit or refuse to admit. You can admit into no other. You cannot make the Union, as to the new States, what it is not as to the old; for then it is not *this* Union that you open for the entrance of a new party. If you make it enter into a new and additional compact is it any longer the same Union? . . . But it is a State which you are to admit. What is a *State* in the sense of the Constitution? It is not a State in general, but a State you find it in the Constitution. . . . Ask the Constitution. It shows you what it means by a State by reference to the parties to it. It must be such a State as Massachusetts, Virginia, and the other members of the American Confederacy—a State with full sovereignty except as the Constitution restricts it. The whole amount of the argument on the other side is, that you may refuse to admit a new State, and that, therefore, if you admit, you may prescribe the terms. The answer to that argument is, that even if you can refuse, you can prescribe no terms which are inconsistent with the act you are to do. You can prescribe no conditions which, if carried into effect, would make the new State less a sovereign State than, under the Union as it stands, it would be. You can prescribe no terms which will make the compact of Union between it and the original States essentially different from the compact among the original States. You may admit or refuse to admit, but if you admit, you must admit a State in the sense of the Constitution—a State with all such sovereignty as belongs to the original parties; and it must be into *this* Union that you are to admit it, not into a Union of your own dictating, formed out of the existing Union by qualifications and new compacts, altering its character and effect, and making it fall short of its protecting energy in reference to the new State, whilst it requires an energy of another sort—the energy of restraint and destruction."[3]

The Missouri Compromise reinforced the older agreement embodied in the Northwest Ordinance by making it clear to older states that they could not hold the West in a "quasi-provincial status."[4] It also reinforced the proposition that the federal system itself would be undermined if the Congress could impose limitations upon the new states which would make them lesser legal entities than the older commonwealths.

[3] The original speech is in the *Annals of Congress*, 16 Cong., 1 sess., cols. 389–417. The quotation here cited is taken from Burgess, *The Middle Period*, 84–86.
[4] *Ibid.*, 105.

This inability of the Congress to permanently reduce the powers of a new state as against those possessed by other states has since been upheld by the Supreme Court of the United States. An instance of this can be seen in a case decided in 1883, relating to the state of Illinois, where the Court declared: "Whatever the limitation upon her powers as a government whilst in a territorial condition, whether from the ordinance of 1787 or the legislation of Congress, it ceased to have any operative force, except as voluntarily adopted by her, after she became a State of the Union." "She was admitted, and could be admitted, only on the same footing with the original states."[5]

The states are, in fact, equal in their political authority. And this equality is the condition of the survival of the federal system. It is true, of course, that the powers of the federal government have greatly expanded in recent years, largely due to the interpretations of the commerce and welfare clauses of the Constitution. But this increase of the powers of the federal government was by consent of the Congress, and affects all of the states equally. It has set no discrimination between one state and another. Furthermore, the states could, by a constitutional amendment, were they so minded, recover whatever part of the powers of the federal government which has accrued to it in recent years.

In the American federal system, therefore, there can be no member of lesser dignity or lower status. Legally,

[5] *Escanaba Co.* v. *Chicago*, 107 U.S. 678, 688, 689 [1883]. Quoted in Andrew C. McLaughlin's *A Constitutional History of the United States* (New York, D. Appleton-Century Co., 1936), 378 n. *(See also Coyle* v. *Smith,* 221 U.S. *Reports* [1910], 559ff. " 'This union' was and is a union of states, equal in power, dignity, and authority, each competent to exert that residium of sovereignty not delegated to the United States by the constitution itself. . . .")

they are all endowed with the same kind of independence, possessed of like privileges, and subject to similar limitations and duties. The differences between the states are measured by size, population, resources, and wealth, and not by status and privilege. There are within our federal system no high and no low, and no great and no lesser states.

This description of the place of each separate state in the United States can be applied to the position of each nation within the Pan-American system. The differences between the United States and the Pan-American system are very great. The first is a nation with a central government, the other is a loose organization resting upon the consent of its members. But each separate entity of either structure in relation to the other members is very much the same.

In the Pan-American system (The Organization of American States as it is now called), each nation is legally equal to any other. Every member nation has one vote. There is no veto. There are no privileged nations grouped in a council possessed of powers denied to the other members. The charter of the organization guarantees each nation its territorial integrity, its sovereignty and independence. No nation or group of nations may intervene in any way in the internal or external affairs of any nation in this hemisphere. All international issues that arise between the member states "shall be settled by peaceful procedures," and attack upon one member is an attack upon all the others. No nations may use economic or political pressure to "force the sovereign will" of any other state for the purpose of gaining some advantage to itself. The territory of each member nation is inviolable, and no territorial acquisitions or other privileges gained by force or other coercion are recognized. All members have an equal place on all of the important committees of the organization and decisions are, in most instances, made by an absolute majority, in a few by a two-thirds vote.

In commenting on the relationship which exists between the nations in this hemisphere, Dr. Alberto Lleras, formerly president of Colombia and recent secretary general of the Organization of American States, had this to say: "Those nations have enjoyed, and will continue to enjoy the inestimable advantage of being neighbors to one of the greatest empires in all history without suffering the fear of imperialism or the threat of violence, basking in an international order based on law which preserves their independence and guarantees their security and sovereignty more fully with each passing day."[6]

After pointing out that equality of voting power, democratic procedure, and majority decisions characterize the working methods of the Organization of American States, Dr. Lleras added, "The same fundamental principle that guides the political life of this country (the United States) prevails in the basic rule of the Organization of American States." Clearly enough, the sixty-year-old organization that includes the twenty-one nations of this hemisphere has gradually acquired increasing power and prestige and has developed greater unity and identity. The charter itself speaks of the "spiritual unity" of the continent. This achievement was a matter of slow growth. But that it has grown to its present role and future promise is due to the acceptance of the principle that nations may differ in size, population, resources, and power, but that they are alike in dignity and status, possessed of equal privileges and bound by equal duties. The

[6] *The Results of Bogota, Lecture Series on the Bogota Conference,* May 24, 25, and 26, 1948, Washington, D. C., 4.

Foreign Minister of Guatemala, Dr. Manuel Salich, expressed the basis upon which the Pan-American system has survived—the older ideal of the co-ordinate state, "... here ... geographic, economic and other differences do not count, ... and ... our voice, which is that of a small country ... has, thanks to the generosity of the other twenty Republics, the same moral rank as the rest...."[7]

If the ideals of the co-ordinate state lie at the base of our own federal system and of the Organization of American States as well, they have also come to play the chief role in the development of the Commonwealth of Nations. It is interesting to note that, at about the period of the American Revolution when James Wilson, Benjamin Franklin, Thomas Jefferson, and James Madison were asserting the doctrine that each colony was co-ordinate under the Crown and legislatively independent of Parliament, some English publicists were advocating similar ideas as a basis for the reconstruction of the British Empire.[8] Major John Cartwright, in a series of letters addressed to Parliament in 1774, pleaded for a reform of the British imperial system on substantially the same grounds as those urged by the leaders of the American colonists. He believed that the empire consisted of a group of states "equal in constitutional status," with co-ordinate legislatures and a common king.[9] The relations between the American colonists and the mother country, he said, were similar to those between Hanover and Great Britain, or between Scotland and England before 1707. He argued, "I would consider the American govern-

[7] Fourth Meeting of Consultation of Ministers of Foreign Affairs, Washington, D. C., *Proceedings, Conference and Organization Series Number 12*, 193.

[8] Robert Livingston Schuyler, *The Fall of the Old Colonial System* (New York, Oxford University Press, 1945) 55–63.

[9] *Ibid.*, 50.

ment, like that of Ireland, as a sister kingdom; and I would cement a lasting union between them as between separate branches of one great family."[10] He wanted the colonies "to be free and independent states" with the king to remain sovereign "in like manner" as he is of Great Britain. He wanted them to be individually and collectively protected against every foreign power and each guaranteed in their independence with respect to the other colonies. He also urged a treaty to establish a perpetual League of Friendship for mutual security against all other states. This change would be of great advantage to the Empire, for then the king would "receive fifteen independent kingdoms in exchange for as many dependent, and *hardly dependent* provinces, and become the father of three million of free and happy subjects, instead of reigning joint tyrant over so many discontented slaves or losing by revolt so many of his people."[11]

Similar ideas were advanced by Granville Sharp, the famous abolitionist, who in 1774 urged in a pamphlet that the permanent recognition of separate legislative power for each colony ought to be adopted because they would then, with the mother country, "form one vast Empire, which will never be divided" because the maintenance of the British constitution inviolate in all the colonies would provide "a sufficient bond of union" between the imperial Crown of Great Britain and the overseas colonies."[12]

Another proponent of similar views was the widely known radical, Dr. Richard Price, who propounded his ideas in the "Observations on the Nature of Civil Liberty, the Principles of Government, and the Justice and Policy of the War with America," published in 1776. Professor

[10] *Ibid.* Quoted by Schuyler, 58.
[11] *Ibid.* Quoted, 59–60.   [12] *Ibid.*, 60–61.

Schuyler summarizes Dr. Price's views in the following words: "His ideal was a voluntary, co-operative alliance of self-governing states, co-ordinate with each other but united through the Crown."[13]

The ideas advocated by Cartwright, Sharp, and Price are strikingly similar to those that now provide the theoretical groundwork upon which the Commonwealth is made to rest. Winston Churchill gave eloquent expression to this basis of Commonwealth unity while paying tribute to the late King George VI. "There is no doubt that of all the institutions which have grown up among us over the centuries or sprung into being in our lifetime, the constitutional monarchy is the most deeply founded and dearly cherished by the whole association of our peoples. In the present generation, it has acquired a meaning incomparably more powerful than anyone had dreamed possible in former times. The Crown has become the mysterious link, indeed I may say the magic link, which united our loosely bound but strongly interwoven Commonwealth of nations, states and races. Peoples who would never tolerate the assertions of a written constitution which implied any diminution of their independence are the foremost to be proud of their loyalty to the Crown. We have been greatly blessed amid our many anxieties and in the mighty world that has grown up all around our small island, we have been greatly blessed that this new, intangible, inexpressible, but, for practical purposes, apparently all-powerful element of union, should have leapt into being among us."[14]

It required the American independence, the difficulties in Canada that led up to the Durham Report in 1839, the slow growth of constitutional federalism in Canada,

[13] *Ibid.*, 62.
[14] *New York Times*, February 8, 1952.

Australia, and New Zealand, the tragedies of the First
World War, the bloody strife in Ireland, and the stubborn, nonresistant movement in India before these ideas
could come into their own.

The change that has occurred is reflected in the new
name for the old British Empire. It came to be called the
British Commonwealth of Nations and more recently,
just the Commonwealth. The Commonwealth is, therefore, composed of formerly subject peoples. These have
now become completely independent nations joined in a
voluntary association, each enjoying the fullest sovereignty and complete equality of rights. Great Britain is,
in fact, only the older member of the Commonwealth and
having the greater prestige and moral authority that has
come to it from age, experience, and a great historical
role. It can make no law for, nor veto one made by its
former dominions; the members of the Commonwealth
have no compulsory allegiance to Britain. A member of
the Commonwealth can, as Eire did during the Second
World War, remain neutral, deny the use of its ports
to the Allied navy, continue diplomatic relations with the
enemy, and still be considered a member of the Commonwealth. The members of the Commonwealth pay neither
tribute nor taxes to Britain. They control their own foreign affairs, have their own diplomatic representatives,
their own armed forces, and make their own immigration
policies. A member nation can secede and break its ties
with the Commonwealth, as Burma has done, or remain
within the Commonwealth and become a republic, as
India has done. The connection between the members
does not rest upon a written constitution or a formal body
of law. It would even be difficult to discover a fully docu-
mented theory that would describe the association. It is
neither a nation nor a formal federation.

But it is not a mere collection of independent units. It is a flexible association of nations, capable of showing great strength and loyalty in a crisis.

Similarly, Switzerland is a federation composed of members possessed of identical legal status. The twenty-five cantons of the Swiss Federation differ greatly in size. Grisons, for instance, has an area of 2,746 square miles, and Zug of 93, while Bern has an estimated population of 729,000, and Uri only 27,000. These twenty-five cantons have varying forms of government, and the 3,164 communes of which they are comprised retain large degrees of home rule. The federal government based on the constitution of 1848, which was strongly influenced by that of the United States, has only limited powers and, by more recent constitutional changes, federal legislation is subject to rejection and modification by popular referendum and initiative. The Swiss cantons have reserved for themselves more of their powers of government than the states of the United States. Federalism in Switzerland dates back to the Alliance between the three forest districts, Uri, Schwyz, and Unterwolden in 1291. Other districts gradually adhered to the original three and, in spite of a turbulent and warlike history, the principle of federalism survived all vicissitudes. For centuries, general affairs were determined by a Diet composed of ambassadors acting under instructions. For nearly six hundred years, the original members of the federation abided by the rule that all disputes between them should be settled by arbitration. Other members gradually joined the original league; Lucerne in 1332, Zurich in 1351, Slarus and Zug in 1352, Bern in 1353. As early as 1481, at the Diet of Stans, the principle of collective security was adopted in the resolution that they would come to the aid of a member attacked by another member. In 1815, the principle of absolute political equality of the cantons was embodied in alloting one vote to each canton, and the territorial integrity of each secured by prohibiting the attack of one member by another. Switzerland stands as the oldest, and in some ways, the most successful federation in the Western world.

The history of the four widely different federations we have just discussed merits careful scrutiny by the student of international organization, for they each, in their own way, illustrate the principle of the co-ordinate state. They also make it clear that the acceptance of that principle is necessary to the growth and survival of a federal system. In the case of the United States, the debate ending in the Missouri Compromise reaffirmed the original proposition that all states stand in relation to each other as equals; that the older states could not sell "a provincial status" to a new state without undermining the foundations of the Union itself. This decision reaffirmed the earlier agreements on an equal vote in the Senate regardless of size of population, on nonintervention by one state in the affairs of another through the provision for judicial settlement of disputes between states, on territorial integrity established in the rule that no state could be divided or united with another against its own will, and that the states reserve all of their powers not deposited in the federal government by the Constitution. The federal government is thus an indestructible union of indestructible states.

Similarly, in the case of the Organization of American States, it was necessary to reaffirm the co-ordinate position of each nation before the Pan-American system could move forward to become a cohesive international body. That reaffirmation required the surrender of the right to intervention in the internal or external affairs for any reason whatsoever, the guaranteeing of the territorial integrity and the political independence of each member nation, the assertion of the principle of collective security, and the affirmation of political and juridical equality which could only be fulfilled by the outlawing of intervention. And, as in the case of the United States, that all disputes between members "shall be settled by peaceful means."

These same conditions have come to define the relations between the members of the Commonwealth of Nations. It is an association of equally independent and sovereign states. There are no great and no lesser members.[15]

The Imperial Conference of 1926 agreed that the dominions and Britain were "equal in status, in no way subordinate to one another in any respect of their domestic or external affairs. . . . Equality of status so far as Great Britain and the dominions are concerned is thus the root principle governing our inter-Imperial relations."[16]

In February, 1948, the Ceylon Independence Act declared that India was "a fully responsible member of the British Commonwealth of Nations, in no way subordinate in any aspect of domestic or external affairs, freely associated and united by a common allegiance to the Crown."[17]

But in South Africa, "the King for purpose of reigning in and over the Union is created by our statutes. . . . The King is, therefore, the King of South Africa and not

[15] *The British Commonwealth and World,* ed. by Richard Frost (London, Royal Institute of International Affairs, 1947), 19.

[16] Quoted in Nicholas Manseigh's *The Commonwealth and the Nations* (London, Royal Institute of International Affairs, 1948), 33.

[17] *Ibid.*

of the Commonwealth. But the Crown has not a 'vestige' of functional reality."[18]

In Ireland, the symbolic character of the Crown proved unacceptable and the oath was repudiated because it was, according to Mr. de Valera, "an intolerable burden."[19] The Irish preferred to be "externally associated." Mr. de Valera declared, "We are associated with the State of the British Commonwealth of Nations. We are not members of it."[20]

To Burma, however, the idea of remaining even as an associate of a British Commonwealth proved unacceptable because they considered that the word "British" implied ownership or subjugation. In 1947, Mr. Thankin Nu, the Burmese prime minister, said that they were, however, prepared to consider association with a united Commonwealth. The change of name was made in 1948 in the Amendment to the British Nationality Act, but it was then too late.[21]

The demand for independent sovereignty of the members of the Commonwealth, which was first fully manifested by the Irish in 1921, who then wanted "external association," but have since fully separated themselves from the Commonwealth, has been completely fulfilled. The concept of dominion status, of a "British" Commonwealth, of the Crown as an essential symbol of unity for all members, have been rejected. The Commonwealth is a free association among completely sovereign states held together by tradition, common historical experience, interest, convenience, and a belief that an

[18] *The Adaptable Commonwealth,* ed. by F. H. Soward, *Proceedings of the Fourth Unofficial Commonwealth Relations Conference,* September 8–18, 1949 (London, Royal Institute of International Affairs, 1950), 3–4.

[19] Manseigh, *The Commonwealth and the Nations,* 201.

[20] *Ibid.,* 202.   [21] *Ibid.,* 11.

association of nations with so much of a common history between them has a bond that is stronger than that which rests upon force or upon a symbol which for reasons of past resentment is unacceptable to some of the members. Unity here lies in freedom and identity. It has been a slow process to convert a world-wide Empire into a free association. But the fact that such a change was possible reflects the resiliency of English constitutional traditions. The milieu of the twentieth century made the symbols of dominion over other peoples incompatible with the passionate nationalism that has dominated our time. The insistent assertion by every people across the face of the earth of a "historical personality" which must not be denied or impugned has made imperialism or even the mere trimmings of foreign rule unacceptable. If the association of many nations, races, and cultures which the British Empire represented was not to break up in hatred and strife, then the constitutional design that would hold them together had to be accommodated both to the political realities of the times as well as to the emotional overtones which they reflect. But once the reconciliation between the older ideas of Empire and the more recent belief in the free "historical personality" has been achieved, then the association finds a sounder and more flexible basis of co-operation than it had before. For now all the associates are equal members of the same family. They are all inside the same house. They are strong with a strength that comes from moral identity and voluntary adhesion. In comparison, a military alliance resting on a balance of power is a rope of sand. On a much smaller scale, and differently, the Swiss Federation has found a similar unity based upon a recognition of diversity of race and language, differences of constitutional forms, and varying historical traditions.

It will be objected that the use of the United States and Switzerland as examples of international organization distorts the meaning of the word "international." It ought, however, to be clear by now that what saved the American federation and made it the kind of organization it is, is precisely the acceptance of the principle of identical sovereignty of the several states among themselves. If the Missouri Compromise had gone differently, our federal system would have gone with it, and the Union, if one had survived, would have been a centralized government plagued with the very difficulties of empire we have just been considering. The same is, of course, also true of Switzerland. The long federal history of that remarkable nation illustrates in a hundred crucial points the vitality of the principle of equal status. And not until that was finally and fully accepted for all cantons did the country settle down to a peaceful political history. It is, therefore, the same principle which operates in all of these four instances of successful international organization, based upon the idea of the co-ordinate states.

In the American point of view, the concept of the co-ordinate state is a general principle of universal applicability. Otherwise, how explain our ceaseless penchant for international organization. The Continental Congress, the United States, the Organization of American States, the League of Nations, the United Nations, the North-Atlantic Treaty Organization, and the effort to stimulate a European union are all parts of the same story. In each instance, there is visible the ideal of co-operation among equal states. How congenial that concept is to the American experience is illustrated at the very beginning of our history, not only by the doctrine of equal legislative sovereignty for the colonies advanced by the early leaders as a proper basis for the organization of the British Empire, but in Benjamin Franklin's suggestion after the formation of the American Constitution that Europe follow our example and establish for itself a federal system. Benjamin Franklin was sagacious and experienced beyond most men, and he knew not only the United States, but had deep knowledge of England and the Continent, and in the ripeness of his years, after helping frame the American Constitution, he felt that it represented a political system that Europe might well adopt for itself. In the year 1787, Franklin wrote to a European friend: "I send you enclosed the proposed new Federal Constitution for these States. I was engaged four months of the last summer in the Convention that formed it. . . . If it succeeds, I do not see why you might not in Europe carry the project of Good Henry the 4th into execution, by forming a Federal Union and One Grand Republic of all its different States and Kingdoms; by means of a like Convention, for we had many interests to reconcile."[22]

The concept of federalism is, with the American people, bred in the bone as part of the idea of political freedom. We believe that security rests upon co-operation, that co-operation is only possible among equals, that equality eliminates the basic reason for political disruption because equals politically are co-ordinate in dignity and in rank, that this common identity is essential for different states to achieve that unity which makes them members of the same political family. International co-operation, from our point of view, requires that all participating members be insiders, and that such a fellowship is, in the end, an "indestructible union." That is why

[22] October 22, 1787, to Mr. Grand. *Documentary History of the Constitution of the United States of America*, Dept. of State, IV (1905), 341–42.

the concept of a balance of power is alien and repugnant to the American people. We have condemned in others the policies derived from that concept and have rejected them for ourselves. Illustrative of this attitude is President Wilson's statement: "The centre . . . of the old order was that unstable thing which we used to call 'balance of power' . . . a thing determined by the sword . . . thrown in on one side or the other; . . ."[23] and "if the future had nothing for us but a new attempt to keep the world at a right poise by a balance of power, the United States would take no interest, because she will join no combination of power that is not the combination of all of us."[24] But to the advocates of power politics and the balance of power, these American convictions and beliefs derived from their own experience are ". . . intoxication with moral abstractions . . . which . . . has become the prevailing substitute for political thought."[25] And Wilson, because he advocated a League of Nations, was driven to "substituting for the concrete national interest of the United States the general postulate of a brave new world where the national interest of the United States, as that of all other nations, would disappear in a community of interests comprising mankind."[26]

These same errors were committed by the leaders of the Second World War, Roosevelt and Hull. The reason for their failure is simple and obvious. "How could statesmen who boasted that they were not 'believers in the idea of balance of power'—like a scientist not believing in the law of gravity—and who were out 'to kill pow-

[23] Albert Shaw, *Messages and Papers of Woodrow Wilson* (New York, Review of Reviews Corporation, 1924), 584.

[24] *Ibid.*, 591.

[25] Hans J. Morgenthau, *In Defense of the National Interest* (New York, A. A. Knopf, 1951), 4.

[26] *Ibid.*, 26.

er politics,' understand the very idea of the national interest which demanded, above all, protection from the power of others?"[27] The American mind has been "weakened in its understanding of foreign policy by half a century of ever more complete intoxication with moral abstractions."[28] The difficulty with American foreign policy is that it is burdened with "utopianism, legalism, sentimentalism [and] neoisolationism."[29] It does not understand that: "Foreign policy, like all politics, is in its essence a struggle for power, waged by sovereign nations for national advantage. . . . By its very nature this struggle is never ended, for the lust for power, and the fear of it, is never stilled. . . . In the life of nations peace is only respite from trouble—or the permanent peace of extinction."[30]

Our great mistake was to assume that the United Nations could be a substitute for the balance of power. We defined it in "Utopian terms of permanent peace and non-competitive, trustful co-operation among the great powers." American policy is wrong because it is interested in the "well-being of all mankind."[31]

A nation is under no obligation to keep a treaty. It is, in fact, an "iron law of international politics that legal obligations must yield to the national interest. . . ." There is apparently no difference between nations that "have a flair for throwing burdensome obligations overboard in an elegant, unobtrusive fashion, or of chiseling them away with the fine tools of legal misinterpretation" like France has done, and Russia and Germany, who "have the disconcerting habit . . . of . . . announcing . . . that a treaty has become a 'scrap of paper.' " These matters are, after all, only "the lawyers' concern" which the states-

[27] *Ibid.*, 32–33.   [28] *Ibid.*, 39.   [29] *Ibid.*, 92.
[30] *Ibid.*, 92.   [31] *Ibid.*, 114.

man can take in his stride in pursuit of the "national interest." Nor need the great powers be concerned about the interests of third parties . . . "great powers . . . have by tradition and logic . . . settled their disputes . . . over the regions where their interests, power and responsibilities were paramount." The business of statesmanship could not be carried on any other way.[32]

It is a legalistic illusion to believe that the United Nations is a substitute for power politics because it is obvious ". . . from the political history of the human race that the balance of power and concomitant spheres of influence are of the very essence of international politics. They may be disregarded at the peril of those who choose to do so but they cannot be abolished."[33] American policy, therefore, operates with "defective intellectual equipment."[34]

Our difficulties derive from our failure to recognize that the balance of power is as much a law of politics as gravity is a law of physics and is illustrated by all of human history. This law, which apparently is basic to the "science" of international relations, has been understood by all the great statesmen, who each in turn have successfully ruined their nations and made a shambles out of all those parts of the world where they have been free to work out the "law" and practice the "science." Now we too, who have prospered by refusing to apply the science or believe in its basic law, are urged, on grounds of the "national interest," to join the historical procession to national suicide by dividing the world between Russia and ourselves. The fact that it runs counter to every political instinct of the American people merely proves that we are possessed of a "defective intellectual equipment," and if we consider it immoral and contrary to our expe-

[32] *Ibid.*, 142–46.   [33] *Ibid.*, 154–55.   [34] *Ibid.*, 159.

rience to trade away the independence and freedom of other nations as part of the bargain, it shows we are sentimental, moralistic, Utopian, and neoisolationists, and we can only refuse to take this advice at our own peril because the balance of power, like the law of gravity, will work its way regardless of what foolish men may do.

Now we submit that all this has nothing to do with science, and little to do with the infinitely complex influences that have shaped the history of man through time. We suspect that it is a very subjective and private view of the nature of man and of his role on earth. And that view seems to be that man is now and has always been in a sad estate from which he cannot extricate himself. He has no one to help him. He has no law to live by, no morality to support him—he has nothing except the balance of power—and if he will not believe in that, then God help him—but in this view of the world, even that comfort is denied to man, for it could not abide any concept of a teleological universe. The interesting thing about all of this is that it should either remain oblivious to or scorn the vast record of co-operative experience among men and nations, and that it should treat the relatively short and exceptional history of the European state system as equivalent to the history of the race across the face of time, and that it should deny the possibility and presumably the desirability of institutional development in the relations between nations. Institutions are presumably, by some undivulged "law," confined to grow only inside of the "sovereign" state. There must be no extra-national institutions; they would deny the "national interest" and make for "a brave new world," which is the greatest of political sins.

There is another statement of this theme of *real-politik* and the balance of power that comes from the influential and highly skilled pen of Mr. George F. Kennan.[35] In this exposition of the case, there is a kind of urbanity, a kind of sensitivity for the values and short-comings of the American milieu, and a kind of compassion for human frailty that robs it of much of its sting. It is so gently, so persuasively stated, that the reader finds himself carried along almost to the point of agreement until he realizes that this modest and restrained presentation is, in fact, a repudiation of every value we hold:

"I see the most serious fault of our past policy formulation to lie in something that I might call the legalistic-moralistic approach to international problems. This approach runs like a red skein through our foreign policy of the last fifty years. It has in it something of the old emphasis on arbitration treaties, something of the Hague Conferences and schemes for universal disarmament, something of the more ambitious American concepts of the role of international law, something of the League of Nations and the United Nations, something of the Kellogg Pact, something of the idea of a universal 'Article 51' pact, something of the belief in World Law and World Government."[36]

This is more than a challenge to our international policies of the last fifty years. It is a denial of the American beliefs that have sustained American political life from the beginning. For our ideas of foreign policy are part and parcel of our belief in human freedom, in the equality of men, and in the dignity and independence of nations. The extenuating feature of Mr. Kennan's presentation is its lack of consistency. There is internal evidence that the author has not really made up his mind

[35] George F. Kennan, *American Diplomacy 1900–1950* (Chicago, University of Chicago Press, 1951).
[36] *Ibid.*, 95.

about these important matters. He is still ambivalent and groping for the truth, and the balance of power has not achieved the status of a "law," like the law of gravity. This is, in our view, a saving grace—but the damage has been done, for an influential voice has been added to the attempt to persuade the American people that their traditional policy based upon the co-ordinate state is wrong and should be abandoned.

The proof often presented by those who would force us off our beaten path is the failure of the League of Nations. A particular instance is made to serve the ends of a universal law. The League having failed, then all international organizations must fail. But the reasons for the failure were numerous, and in our view, the fact that it was not based upon the idea of the co-ordinate state was one of its major weaknesses. It can surely be argued that the principle of collective security failed under the League of Nations precisely because the League was not built upon the principle of the co-ordinate state. If all the members of that body had had an equal voice, Italy's attack upon Ethiopia would have been defeated, and sanctions, both economic and military, would have been effectively applied.

It will be said in reply the small powers would here have committed the large ones to a possible war in which they would have borne a minor part. That may or may not be true. But the way to have avoided the greater tragedy which ultimately destroyed or weakened both the great as well as the small states was to have acted as the small states would have acted—to enforce the principle that in the modern world there are no separate interests for the small or the large state, that their destinies are collectively involved in each other, and the violation by war and oppression of the independence of even the smallest power is, in the end, the denial of the possible survival without war even of the largest power. For such violation, whatever the grounds on which it is justified, is in effect the building of aggressive power against other nations until they, too, are placed in jeopardy. In this view of the matter, the structuring of international organization on the co-ordinate state is the alternative to the balance of power, and the means to security without permanent militarization.

Nor must we permit ourselves to be confused by the argument that the United Nations has failed and that the North-Atlantic Treaty Organization is the true substitute. The North-Atlantic Treaty Organization is conceived of as a temporary and instrumental association of a defensive character, organized for the purpose of implementing the ideal of the United Nations. It has nothing to do with the balance of power idea and less to do with dividing the world into spheres of interest between Russia and ourselves. Its objectives are aimed precisely at an attempt to prevent the permanent militarization which dividing the world into spheres of influence would require, and to escape the destruction of the democratic process which would follow in its wake.

The American people will not accept the program. They will not consent to the destruction of all that a hundred and fifty years of democratic life has brought them for the sake of being the masters of that part of the world which they could lay hold of. They will not do it because it runs against their grain, and because they have an alternative which seems more difficult to those hypnotized by the ideal of force and craft, but is, in fact, easier and more consistent with our own traditional way with other people, and one we know how to live with because we have always done so. And that is the gathering of as many nations as we may upon the basis of the co-ordinate state, not for the sake of achieving a balance of power, but for the sake of building a basis of common defense upon a system of collective security open to all the nations of the world who wish to join it, without losing their independence or their dignity.

A balance of power settlement would lead our many allies and associates to conclude that they are mere pawns in a game of international politics, played at their expense. They would cease to be partners in a great cause. For the division of the world into spheres of influence would automatically destroy the basis of the partnership in the West. That partnership rests upon the assumption of equality of the members, that their rights cannot be bargained away, that they have to be consulted, that they have to consent freely to changes that affect them. It also rests upon the assumption that there are *no* spheres of influence—that the United States has no rights greater than the least of its members, and that the defense is a joined defense of a common interest, but that the common interests rests upon the particular and unique political personality of each member. It assumes a co-ordinate relationship, not the position of a great power with a lot of satellite powers. The mere acceptance of the idea of a balance of power would undermine the basis of voluntary association among free partners and convert it into an empire with satellites to be ordered about. It would convert the United States from a federal Republic to an empire and ultimately destroy the Republic. That is what the proposal really means, and that is why it will be resisted by the American people.

Such an arrangement would lead our friends to fall away from us feeling that they had been betrayed, as in fact, they would have been. They, too, would seek the best bargain—temporarily, and play for higher stakes when the occasion offered. We would find ourselves weaker in the international field, not stronger. We would have voluntarily accepted a great moral defeat, and the power derived from a common cause among nations, all of whom felt identified through interest, belief, and outlook, would have been irretrievably lost. The only remaining hope that an association of co-ordinate states could be gathered together to resist the attempt by Russia to dominate the world would evaporate. It is difficult to foresee a day more dark and hopeless than the one on which American people could be persuaded to seek a temporary peace through deliberately sacrificing the principle of voluntary association among nations, and agree to divide the world between Russia and ourselves.

No. With all of our shortcomings and failings, we will not accept the new science and follow the "will-of-the-wisp" of *realpolitik*. We will not abandon the faith we have lived by, nor deny the other nations the right to live in freedom and without fear. Our commitments are to a world of free men working together in free nations. The democratic faith that lies at the basis of everything we cherish is the overriding law of American policy both at home and abroad. We cannot surrender our belief in the equal dignity of little nations without in the end abandoning our belief in the equal dignity of man. We will, if we have to, resist to the death the effort to subvert the world to a totalitarian despotism, but we will not bargain with it at the expense of other people and to the destruction of that sense of human integrity and national morality which is part of the substance of our very being. This may not be "science," but that is the way it is. We can do no other. Therein lies our strength.

Index